The Find

To Ian & family,
With love,
Verica Peacock
April 2006

The Find

The Story of a War Child
by VERICA PEACOCK

Central Publishing Services
West Yorkshire

Cover photograph: Verica (1) and Marijana on delivery from the orphanage in wartime Zagreb.

Paperback ISBN 1 904908 31 4
www.vericathefind.info

Produced
by

Central Publishing Services.
Royd Street Offices
Milnsbridge
Huddersfield
West Yorkshire
HD3 4QY

www.centralpublishing.co.uk

To Graham, with my love

WHETHER I LIVE

Whether I live, or whether I die,
Whatever the worlds I see,
I will come to you by-and-by,
And you will come to me.

Whoever was foolish, we were wise,
We crossed the boundary line,
I see my soul look out of your eyes,
You see your soul in mine.

Mary Coleridge

CONTENTS

POEMS

PHOTOS

FOREWORD

Just like many other people I have, in the past, thought that I would like to write a book encompassing my experiences through life, which has been quite eventful. However, just like most people, I have considered that I was always too busy and put it off until the day when I had time.

Realising at last that, with all the activities with which I always busied myself and the demands of the family, the time might never come, I thought I had better make a start.

A local group of WI members has recently asked me to give them a talk on my life and, after I jotted down some notes, when asked by an old school-friend, I sent them to her. Her response: "After your experiences, what a wonder that the little girl who was you has grown up to be so normal and well balanced", which I took as a great compliment. I feel that we all learn something from each new experience in life, even the negative ones.

Also, when people have asked me about my childhood and adolescence in Croatia, ex-Jugoslavia and heard something about them, they have usually said: "You ought to write a book about your experiences. It sounds more strange than a work of fiction and would make very interesting reading." Therefore, I have now done just that.

November 2004

Reviving memories in Jelačić Square
Summer 2003

CHAPTER 1
My Parents And Changed Circumstances

"Dušo" (doosho), a term my father always used when addressing my mother, even when they were arguing - meaning soul, but equivalent to darling - "I have some shattering news! I'm sorry, but I've lost my job." He then went on to explain that the bank belonging to his cousin, Julius, where he was manager, had been bankrupted that day.

Mama and tata were sitting at their usual table in the cafe on Jelačić Square, where they used to meet most afternoons after he finished work. At any time of day or evening the square and the cafes surrounding it were always full of people. Like the statue of Eros in London, that of Ban Jelačić, the Croatian Baron, who abolished feudalism, was the most popular meeting place in town.

Greeting the news with floods of tears, my mother searched for a handkerchief in her immaculately tidy handbag and proceeded to wipe her eyes. She was speechless at first, realising the implications of this loss. She contemplated our bleak future, instead of trying to console my father.

Brightening slightly, she then took control. "We can move to a smaller flat, give up our house in the centre of the town and I can go to work. I don't care what I do, as long as we have enough money to buy food." Slava, my governess, whom I called 'Vava', was the first to go, followed by our move to a small flat on the first floor of a run down block of flats on the periphery of the town.

Father enjoyed his work and was lost without it. He still spent afternoons in the cafes in the centre, drinking coffee and smoking and possibly playing cards and gambling. He was always a soft touch, which was OK whilst he was earning, but annoyed my mother in our straitened circumstances.

Mother was never afraid of hard work and during the Austro-Hungarian Empire, before the first World War, she worked as secretary for the government, but when she was needed, volunteered to work for the Red Cross. Therefore, she decided that it was no good staying at home and worrying where the next meal was coming from, but found a job selling soap from door to door. When that did not bring in enough money, she obtained a job demonstrating gadgets, make up and anything suitable at the exhibitions regularly held in Zagreb. Several times a year large exhibitions, similar to the Daily Mail Ideal Home Exhibition were held under the title of Velesajam, a precursor of a modern, permanent Hypermarket, which is its nearest equivalent.

I missed Vava very much and, being only two years old, could not understand why she was with us no more. However, I adapted to living in the new flat very quickly and was pleased that I suddenly had so many friends of my own age or a little older in the other flats in the block. We had a large concrete yard where we played hopscotch, rode our bicycles or hid in the cellar behind stacks of coal. There was always excitement once a month when coal was being delivered and the sacks emptied through the little windows at pavement height straight into the cellar.

The cellar occasionally had an unusual smell, probably some kind of disinfectant, but some of the children and I thought it smelled of dragons and were afraid to play there whilst the smell lasted. I still occasionally get a whiff of that smell and it transports me to that, for me at the time, carefree pre-war era.

As well as coal deliveries, the flats also had regular deliveries of wood, as soon as autumn drew near. I don't know whether whole tree trunks used to be delivered in England at that time, but that was certainly the case in Jugoslavia. We children who were not at school yet - there was no pre-school or nursery school at that time in Zagreb - used to gather around the saw table, only to be shooed away so that we didn't get hurt, in order to catch some of the logs. I can still hear the whine and screech of the saw in my mind and have recently translated a Croatian poem by Dobriša Cesarić called autumn, in which he recalls the same sound. To him and to me the typical whine of the saw cutting through wood signals the imminent arrival of autumn and its attendant misty days.

When my mother had to go out, she usually took me with her if it was possible; for instance, when she hawked soap around, and that is how I learnt to read. I would constantly ask the names of the streets, squares, shops we passed, tram numbers and any other signs with letters and numbers; I would tell her what they were, until I graduated to newspapers. When I discovered my love of reading these, my happiness was complete. Apparently, I would read them from cover to cover, even if I could not understand them, but the oddest phenomenon was the fact that when I finished reading them, I would tear pieces off and eat them. I even remember carrying parcels wrapped in newspapers and eating the paper! I still love reading newspapers, but have better taste in food!

However poor we now were, my mother still took pride in our appearance and I was still one of the best-dressed children in our building, even if most of my clothes were carefully pressed hand me downs from our richer friends and relations. Whenever we went out, my mother would get me ready first, then let me go down to the yard to talk to other children while she got herself ready. No doubt, when I was two and a half years old, I paraded in my neat outfit one particular day, boasting that we were going somewhere special. This was too much for one of my small neighbours, Marijan, who was just a few months older than me. He calmly reached into his short trousers and sprayed me from head to foot. To say my mother was not best pleased when, ready to leave, she had to change me completely, would be an understatement. Never again did she get me ready first!

This scene is so vivid in my mind that I can still almost feel the indignity and remember the clothes I was wearing at the time: a white smocked frock with red polka dots, a huge bow at the back and a white pussycat bow in my dark hair.

Also vivid is my misdemeanour at a birthday party I attended for a friend of a similar age during this period. The custom at the time was for children to take a large box of chocolates as a birthday present and I duly presented my friend with her box of chocolates, on arrival. During the party, apparently, I disappeared into a corner and devoured most of the contents of the box I had given her. When my mother remonstrated, I could not understand why. I kept saying I had shown it to her and the present was the fact that I had brought it. I didn't realise I was not meant to eat it, I thought it was mine! I remember my mother apologising most profusely and promising to buy another box and send it round. Again, the shame I recollect is vivid, despite my very young age.

Now for some details about my parents and more about my early years.

My mother, Elvira, was the youngest of 18 children, although not all of them survived into adulthood. Her mother, Fanny, was eighteen when she married her nineteen years old sweetheart, Marko. They lived frugally, but happily, adding to their family almost yearly, until my mother was born in 1895. By that time, those of my mother's brothers who had survived were grown up, so that my mother felt as if she had several fathers, they were so strict with her and bossed her around. Apparently, when my mother was in her early twenties, my grandmother would ask her if she was still a virgin and would say that she would give her poison if she knew she was not. My mother would tease her and say "Why do you attach so much importance to virginity? If I was not a virgin, would that be worse than if I stole or lied or hurt someone?" This would anger my grandmother and, sometimes, mother's grown up brothers would get a belt to strike her, in order to teach her not to answer her mother back.

The present generation would find all this incomprehensible and I must agree. In any case, how ridiculous to attach more importance to a physical characteristic than to morality!

My grandparents had fourteen boys and four girls and, curiously, after the Second World War, all the four daughters were still alive, whilst all the sons were dead. Unfortunately, mother did not tell me much about her childhood and, now that she is dead, I wish I had talked to her more about it. However, I do remember her laughingly telling me that in the little cafe owned by her parents, she would dance as a little girl, while people threw pennies or, rather, dinars, at her. The other information she volunteered was that, because she was the youngest and her mother's favourite, my grandmother longed for me to be born, so that she could see me but, unfortunately, she died of stomach cancer in my mother's arms in our house just before I was born on 6 March 1930, in the Maternity Clinic in Zagreb.

There could not have been a more ill-matched pair than my mother and father: she, a townie, slightly spoiled, because she was the youngest of many children, he the product of village grocers, the oldest of three boys and four girls, from the small village of Kozice in Croatia.

My Grandparents

My mother's parents, Fanika and Marko

Occasionally, when I was very, very young, I spent summer holidays at my father's parents' village house, enjoying the fresh air and simple life, catching a glimpse of the carefree youth which he must have enjoyed until he left to further his education and then his call up to join the Austro-Hungarian Army and take part in the First World War. That last experience left him with very bad asthma and thrombosis in his legs.

Two of my earliest memories of those holidays in Kozice are, firstly, the large horn of a gramophone on top of the wardrobe, which mesmerised me every afternoon while I was put to rest or sleep on a small divan in my grandparents' bedroom. I was very worried that somehow I would be sucked into the horn and disappear. My second early memory is playing with the duck manure near a pond, which I squeezed through my fingers and watched in fascination as it fell to the ground. Even now I can recall the warmth of the sun's rays reflecting on the duck-pond in the centre of the little village, while I played with the dirt and one of my aunts tried to prevent me from eating it and taking some home. My mother, who was fastidious and pedantic in the extreme was horrified when she heard how I had spent my time!

Being in her late twenties, my mother was apparently feeling she was 'on the shelf', and, as it was often customary in those days, her eldest brother, Albert, was approached, with a view to finding her a suitable prospective husband. Uncle Albert was a very genial cafe proprietor, whose only notable attribute I can remember, apart from great age, or so it seemed to me at the time when I visited him, when I was three years old, was the fact that he had beautiful auburn hair. Our son, Neil, seems to have inherited it.

In common with most of the population of Zagreb then, my father used to spend quite a lot of his time sipping coffee and smoking in uncle Albert's cafe. Therefore, it was not surprising that, when an opportunity arose, uncle introduced my mother to the smart, good-looking young man, Marko Šlezinger, who worked in a bank. They fell in love or, rather, I would like to think that they fell in love, pretty quickly and decided to get married.

Although I know that uncle Albert arranged the marriage, I think they began it in a state of being 'in love'. This might, of course, just be wishful thinking on my part. I know that they never particularly liked each other; my mother especially did not like my father's nature of being too generous and easy-going. He would give away his last penny or shirt to one who spun him a hard luck story, while he himself needed the money. In addition, he was extremely untidy, according to my mother, whereas she was unbelievably and pedantically tidy. A story has been told to me that when she stayed with a friend a button fell off her nightdress in the middle of the night. A soon as it happened, my mother got up, found a needle and cotton and quickly sewed it on. It's a pity I have not inherited this trait!

One thing my mother and father had in common, apart from their youth and religion, was the fact that both had participated in the First World War: he in the trenches, where he was 'gassed' and had his health impaired for the rest of his life, she, as mentioned before, as one of the youngest volunteer nurses in a military hospital, for which she was decorated. I have just passed on to my daughter the silver dog medal, which bore a red cross on its back, which my mother passed on to me when we were reunited after the Second World War.

Mother and father started their married life in a large house in the centre of Zagreb. He was by then the manager of the bank and mother had given up her job as a secretary, in order to become a full time housewife. She became pregnant almost at once but, apparently, wanted to wait a little longer before experiencing motherhood and, therefore, had an abortion, thus depriving me of an older brother. It seems to have been fashionable and easy at that time to have an abortion and my mother's was performed by a doctor who was the husband of one of her friends and was well known for this practice.

Eventually, my mother became pregnant again and this time, it appears, she very much wanted the baby girl born on that cold and frosty morning in March 1930.

At first, everything was wonderful. Although they employed a governess, my mother apparently very proudly used to wheel my pram through Zrinjevac Park in the centre of the town, while people thought she was pushing a doll in place of a real live baby as, according to her, I was supposed to look just like a doll. I used to blush every time she recounted this story when I was in my late teens!

In the afternoons when my father came home from work he would play with me and I remember him as a kindly, good looking man, always saying: "Molim te dušo" (Please, darling), to my mother, entreating her not to be cross about something or other.

When we became poor almost overnight, my father's sister, auntie Jelka, and her husband, uncle Emil, would often buy me clothes and help my parents out. They were childless and uncle Emil had a secure job at the Electricity Board. He used to be a teacher, a profession he loved, but could not follow, as the money earned was not enough for a decent life. As he could buy electrical goods at a discount, uncle Emil and auntie Jelka had the only hairdryer in the family and I remember going to their house for my twice-weekly hair wash or borrowing the drier to bring home.

I must have been very conscious of our reduced circumstances, because many years later auntie Jelka reminded me that she once asked me what I would do if someone gave me a sum of money. I replied that I would, first of all, give my mother money for rent, then my father money to pay back all he owed, pay for the coal, buy groceries for a month and then, if there was anything left, buy myself a book or a toy. I was about three years old at the time, she said.

Another sign of our frugality was my mother's excuse for her cakes always being very small. "Please excuse the size of the cakes", she would say to visitors, "but Verica will only eat them if they are small." The real reason, of course, was that there were more cakes in number, the smaller they were.

My mother and father began to go their separate ways at around this time. Tata, as I called my father - it is the Croatian equivalent of daddy - would come home late at night, full of wonderful plans how we would be rich again. He gambled at cards and, according to my mother, usually lost. Mama, on the other hand, always much more practical than my father, carried on earning money by doing temporary jobs, which other people usually shunned.

That winter I spent more and more time in our flat teaching myself to read and write in earnest using the implements prevalent in infant schools at that time, a slate and chalk. My mother wanted me to wait and learn these skills at school, but I said that if she would not teach me, I would teach myself. This was helped by the lettering on street names and the numbering on tramways, as mentioned before. Tramways were the mode of transport in Zagreb then and are still nowadays, although they have now been supplemented by buses. Unfortunately, these days there are no disciplined queues for getting on either trams or buses; it's everyone for himself or herself, but usually all manage to get on. Both buses and trams run very frequently.

There has been some research done on earliest memories of children and it is difficult to ascertain whether any particular memories are one's own or whether they are the result of assisted recall, or even the result of the child hearing parents or relatives relating the same occurrences over and over again. Although I can remember clearly in great detail all my life from the age of four, I can also clearly recall the incident in the yard of the tenement building when I was much younger.

I still harboured a grudge against little Marijan for watering me that day when I was smartly dressed with a pretty red bow in my hair and bided my time until I could have my revenge. It came when I was about three. Coal and firewood were being delivered that day and the cellar door was open, while the coal bunkers for each flat were unlocked. I carefully lured Marijan inside, promising him sweets. When he was inside the coalbunker, I padlocked the door and went upstairs to lunch, telling nobody. After lunch I was put to rest as usual, until my father came home in the afternoon around 3 o'clock. When he came to see me, he quietly reproached me: "Verica, how could you be so naughty as to lock Marijan in the cellar? Do you know, he has only just got out!"

My reply: "If I had known he would ever get out, I would not have considered it worth while locking him up", elicited the first and only beating with a belt that I had ever known from my father or, indeed, anyone else. My father said that if I had shown remorse and apologised, he would have accepted this, but my wickedness in saying what I did, deserved a beating.

I did only one other wicked thing in my life as far as those who know me and I remember. Together with a few others, I pushed a girl through the small window into the cellar, splitting her head open. Why we did that I don't remember, only the guilt and fear of repercussions has stayed with me. Quite mistakenly, I thought at that time that this was the trigger, which caused my life to be drastically changed.

Despite these two misdemeanours, people say that I was very kind and generous to everyone and would give my last sweet to a friend.

Another incident, but pleasant, happened at around this time, whilst I was wearing my favourite red, double-breasted coat with gold buttons. A big boy (at least twelve years old), Milivoj, gave me a present of a colouring book and sweets, beautifully wrapped, together with a bunch of flowers. I felt so very grown up!

The only advantage of living in our reduced circumstances was the fact that our small flat was near Zagreb's famous Zoo in Maksimir and occasionally I was taken to see the animals there. We would take a picnic with us and summers always seem to have been warm and sunny. In fact, I never remember rainy days before the war, only sunshine or snow!

The biggest attraction in the Zoo were the brown and polar bears, who always looked as tame as my teddies. It was good that I could see animals occasionally, as we were not allowed to keep pets in the flat. In fact, I don't remember anyone I knew having a pet. The frst pets I came into contact with were the puppy, Lady, a Cocker Spaniel, and my cat Zaza, both of which were given to me by Uncle Rudi. Of, course, I adored both my animals. We had Lady for years and I remember her lovely litter of puppies, all of whom we gave away to friends. Unfortunately, Lady lost her figure after that and became very fat, though still lovable.

According to my mother, I was a very finicky eater. I would take hours over eating any meal and had an appetite as small as a bird's. However, as soon as we were visiting someone, I would start by saying: "Mama, I'm very hungry!" The hostess would then give me cakes or even bread and butter, which would always taste much better than at home and I would demolish the lot quickly. It must have been very embarrassing for my mother.

It sounds to me as if I was a spoiled, precocious brat, though my family deny this. Perhaps it was because of our misfortune, that both my parents showered all their love on to me, when they could no longer share their love with each other.

When my parents decided to separate and the incident with the girl we pushed into the cellar occurred, I was four and a half years old and my mother seriously started to consider an offer made by her favourite brother, Rudi and his wife, Marga, who were childless. Uncle Rudi was an eminent barrister in a small town called Slavonski

Brod. He and auntie Marga lived in a spacious house with gardens and owned a vineyard in the mountains on the outskirts of Brod. They were desperate to have children but, apparently, auntie Marga could not have any. Therefore, when my parents decided to part, my mother accepted her brother's and sister-in-law's offer to look after me and bring me up as their own. She would not let me be legally adopted, but that was the only stipulation made when she handed me over.

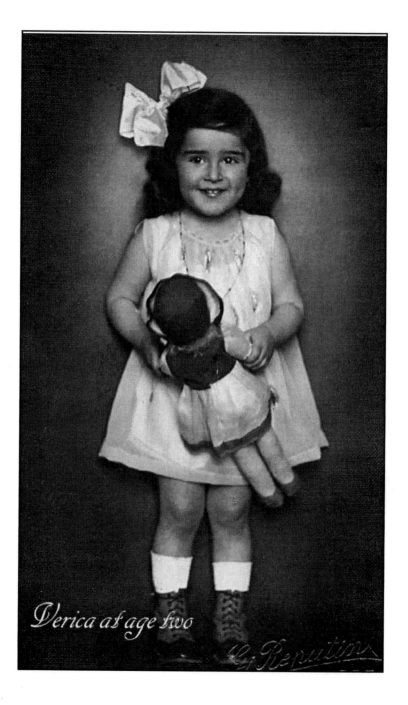

Verica at age two

THE CHILD

Who is this beautiful child
so happy and smartly attired?
Lucky child, on the threshold of life,
doesn't know what fate has in store.
Her eyes are clear like the water
which runs in a mountain spring
now, seventy years later
those eyes can barely see anything.

The old photograph had been mislaid
over many, many decades,
from country to country it travelled
through years, but its beauty never fades.

You can keep bright colours and gimmicks
digital photos and such,
give me a sepia print of old
whose memory means so much.

Who is this beautiful child
whose gaze beguiles each beholder,
whose life could no one predict?
That child, who was captured in time,
but vanished like a flickering flame,
who evokes such visions of the past
when life was just a game -
is no one else, but me!

CHAPTER 2
Change Of Environment

At first I thought it was for only a few days or weeks that I would remain in Brod, but gradually it dawned on me that it would be, more or less, for ever, and I was quite happy about it.

It always surprises me how adaptable and resilient children are. Show them some kindness, provide them with physical comforts and sustenance and they can be yours forever, momentarily forgetting, or placing in the background of their minds, their real parents. I never forgot mine, occasionally receiving or writing them letters but, at least until my teens and deprivation brought about by my circumstances, I hardly ever mentioned them or thought much about them. In fact, I think I regarded them as remote figures who loved me and whom I loved, but who were always busy and somehow out of reach.

From the day I arrived in Brod, I felt at home. I quickly settled down to life there, enjoying every minute of it. Although I always called them auntie Marga and uncle Rudi, they were the best parents anyone ever had, who took me out for meals at least once a week, when the local inn would roast either a lamb or a suckling pig on a spit.

My favourite was the lamb, because I could then be given the very crisply barbequed tail, which was delicious. (Still so after a break of 64 years, when I had it in 2004!)

Auntie Marga revelled in the fact that at last she had a child of her own to dress, take out, show off. She had beautiful clothes made for me, the latest fashion for girls, such as flimsy summer dresses in pastel colours with dainty patterns; one particular dress had a small cape attached. When I had to go to a fancy dress party, she had a dress made from satin, as a chequerboard with alternate black/white squares and I won the prize for the best and most unusual costume.

At that time aunt Marga and uncle Rudi had a full time cook, Jelka, who came from Slovenia and was only 19 years old, and a charlady who came in every day for a few hours to clean the house and, sometimes, in the evenings, to help with entertaining our guests, if need be. I loved them both, as they made a lot of fuss of me and Jelka would sometimes play with me, when she had time and often talked to me. In fact, I learnt a lot from her, things I should and maybe should not have done at the tender age of five or six. I remember discussing with her an article I read in the newspaper that a girl of five had had a baby in Lima in Peru and asked her how that could happen. She explained that it said that the little girl started her periods at two and became pregnant at five. Now we know that by its proper name of precocious puberty.

After digesting this information for a little while, I asked Jelka if I was backward, as I still had not had my periods at six! She then put my mind at rest and explained all the rest of the facts of life to me.

Auntie and uncle's vineyard in the hills above Slavonski Brod was very inviting and every Saturday or Sunday we used to go either by taxi or fiacre - a horse drawn carriage - to visit it. At the time, in those pre Second World War days, there was only the actual vineyard there, a wooden privy and a very large shed containing a vine press, tools and deckchairs with a table for eating our picnic food, which our cook had prepared for us. We shared the caretaker with a neighbouring owner and admired all the new villas that sprang up nearby, all the while planning one of our own.

I really enjoyed these excursions, especially as Miloš, our vincilir (caretaker), had three sons and a daughter of my own age, with whom I formed friendships. When I was older, I used to love roaming around the hillside with them, admiring the views of Brod, shopping at the little general store at the foot of our hill. Walking in the fresh air on grass was so much more fun than walking in town on pavements.

In the autumn, when the grapes were ripe, they were pressed and nothing has ever tasted as good or refreshing as the 'most' which came out of our press! I presume the wine made out of those grapes must have been equally as good, as uncle Rudi was very proud of it at his dinner parties.

Around 1938, uncle decided that we ought to have a villa built in our vineyard, in order that we could stay the whole weekend there instead of just going for a day. I remember the day the foundations of the villa were laid. There was great excitement and ceremony. The caretaker and vineyard labourers, together with the builder and his workers toasted my uncle and his family, while we wished them all the best.

Every weekend after that we saw the building take shape. The accommodation consisted of a large enclosed lounge/verandah, with windows all round, my aunt and uncle's bedroom, a spare room, my bedroom, a beautifully fitted large kitchen, bathroom and toilet with running water, unheard of in weekend properties, in those days of outside toilets. As a special favour, I was allowed to choose my own furniture. This I chose all in pink, including a pink headboard with a built in modern bedside cabinet.

There was no electricity in Brodsko Vinogorje - the vineyard-clad hillside above Brod - at the time and we had beautiful oil lamps and candle holders. It is a wonder I did not set the whole place alight one evening when I had a friend to stay and tried to show her how I could get my celluloid hair slide through the flame of a candle without setting it alight. Once, while I did it, it caught fire and I managed to smother it with my pillow.

When the building was completed we, of course, started spending whole weekends there. Eagerly we awaited the taxi on Friday evenings, in order to be whisked almost to another world, full of fresh mountain air, birdsong, cows going home to be milked, for there were farms around, as well as vineyards. I also looked forward to the latest news or gossip to be told to me by Seka, the caretaker's daughter, whose real name was Branka. I smoked my very first and only cigarette there under the vine leaves, when I was about ten years old. It must have have tasted awful, thank goodness, in order for me to be put off smoking for life. If only youngsters of today could be put off smoking so easily, how many lives could be saved?

The journey by taxi took about twenty-five minutes, depending on whether we had to wait any length of time at the railway crossing. We also passed a famous large factory where railway trains and tramways were built, which was one of the biggest employers in our little town.

In those halcyon pre Second World War days none of us imagined that soon the time would come for us to live in our vineyard villa permanently for a while and give up our comfortable large house in Brod, with its servants.

Every month uncle had to attend the District Courts at the nearby towns of Požega and Osijek. He usually took auntie Marga and me on these trips. When we went to Osijek it was always by train, but when we went to Požega it was usually by taxi. The journey by taxi was always broken into two parts: one stop at an inn for a meal of delicious 'sekele goulash'*, and the other stop for me to be car sick and get rid of the meal I had so enjoyed, for I was always sick on any lengthy car journey.

When we visited Osijek, auntie and I enjoyed shopping in this large town, while. uncle was busy at Court. The train journey passed through the very fertile and beautiful countryside of Slavonija, rich in whitewashed little villages, verdant meadows and cornfields, for this part was known as the breadbasket of the country.

At this time, when I was about seven, I acquired two skills of

---

* *a type of stew with Sauerkraut*

which my uncle was especially proud. The first was that I learnt to play cards and became, supposedly, unbeatable, whatever the game, and the second was my skill at playing table-tennis, at which it was also apparently hard to beat me. Whenever we entertained guests and this was very often, I would have to perform. Most people took it in good part to be beaten at both these games by the skill of a seven year old, smaller in stature than average, but I am sure uncle must have lost some friends, who felt it undignified to lose to a precocious child!

My aunt tried to teach me the piano when I was five, but as she had no patience, she frequently lost her temper and bit my arm when I played a wrong note. I was, therefore, quickly transferred to a proper piano teacher.

In ex-Jugoslavia children started school at seven years of age but, as my documents were in Zagreb, I managed to start at six, by pretending I was that age. In any case, by that time I could read and write in two alphabets, Latin and Cyrillic, know something about numbers and was, apparently, quite an asset to the school. I helped to teach other children to read and write, thus taking some burden off the hard working infant teacher.

During those very happy early schooldays, I acquired my very first boyfriend, Zvonko Markotić. He sat next to me in school and for several years we were inseparable, both in and out of school, as he lived only a few doors away from me. We were very evenly matched scholastically and even obtained equal top marks when we sat the equivalent of the 11+ examination (although I was ten at the time).

Zvonko was very tubby, a little like a miniature version of Billy Bunter; his main preoccupation in life was food. I remember my aunt arranging for us to visit a lady, a friend of hers, who was well known for baking delicious cakes. We carefully told Zvonko to accept the very first cake he was offered, to decline politely when offered a second but, if the hostess persisted in offering it again, to accept, if he so desired.

All went according to plan. Zvonko heartily accepted the first cake, which he wolfed down in double quick time. The hostess then offered all of us a second cake, which we politely declined. She then became so engrossed in conversation with my aunt, that she forgot to offer the cakes a third time. Gradually, Zvonko's patience ran out and his fingers kept leaping forward towards the cake stand and backwards towards his empty plate. I sustained my laughter until I could keep it no longer to myself and burst forth. The hostess asked what was wrong. Zvonko replied honestly, explaining in detail how we taught him the rules of etiquette, much to her amusement and my aunt's acute embarrassment.

The high point of the day in Brod was the evening promenade round the town square, the Korso. As soon as it was dusk, everyone who was anyone, particularly teenagers and children, would dress in their best clothes to walk round and round to see and be seen. My friends and I would usually walk with my aunt and uncle, as he was beloved of all young people in the town and was a typical universal uncle. I don't remember ever being jealous, just proud and lucky that I could have him all the time, while they could only enjoy his company and attention on the promenade.

My best friend at that time, apart from Zvonko, was Fela (Felicity), the only daughter of the Jewish Cantor in Brod. I remember learning Hebrew with her and eating kosher meals at her house, whilst she could not eat most of the food at our house, usually pork, ham, etc. I never found out what happened to Fela after the war. I'm sure she perished in some concentration camp or other, together with her family and many of our acquaintances and relatives. Her father's beautifully clear singing voice and Al Jolson looks still haunt me.

Auntie Marga often entertained her friends in the mornings for coffee and liqueurs. The choice of the latter was usually enormous, but she was particularly proud of the two that she used to make:

Advocat and Coffee liqueur. I was allowed to come in and say "Hello" to her lady guests, but was not, of course, allowed to taste any of the drinks. However, I used to sneak into the room when auntie was saying "Good-bye" to her friends and drink the tiny remnants of liqueurs left in their glasses! There could not have been much left in them, as I don't remember ever being drunk or auntie noticing anything unusual about me. In fact, I've never been drunk in my life!

When aunt's female friends came to the house and I was present, but they didn't want me to hear what they were discussing, they would usually speak in French. As I could understand and speak German, that was out of the question. Auntie Marga, like most girls from very rich families before the war, was educated at a Swiss Finishing School and, therefore, spoke excellent French.

There were three people close to us whom we visited often: auntie Marga's father, stepmother, Ella and stepbrother, Fritz. Ella was German or Austrian and that is why her son did not have a Slavonic name. Marga's father was extremely rich, old and quiet, while her stepmother was haughty, bossy and very disdainful. She considered that little girls should only be seen, but never be heard and, although I tried to be well behaved, quiet and polite, I felt I never succeeded in being a model child where she was concerned.

My aunt's father gave her a lot of jewellery throughout her life, including a diamond-studded collar and earrings set, all of which were promised to me when I grew up. As it turned out, of course, by the time I would have inherited them, the German Army and Ustashe had confiscated and dispersed them!

Some of my memories of those days are so weird I can hardly believe they are true. For instance, seeing leeches covering our charlady's arm when she was ill is one memory that has stayed with me, although this, I am sure was unheard of in England in 1937, or was it? Curiously enough, or was it pure synchronicity, a few minutes after I wrote this, I heard on the radio that alternative medicine still uses leeches. Apparently, when fastened on to part of a person's body, they inject something into the blood that increases its viscosity and prevents it from clotting.

I also recall our charlady crying bitterly when her tiny baby grandchild was very ill with meningitis and then died. This was the first corpse I had ever seen and it distressed me greatly to see a tiny, limp baby lying still.

Another vivid memory of that time was my aunt's dressmaker, who used to come to the house to mend our linen. This unfortunate person was a hermaphrodite and I was scared when she came to the house, because the cook and the maid always whispered about her and her appearance, though I do not remember that she looked any different from anyone else.

Meanwhile, my mother and father had separated and, while my father remained in Zagreb, my mother spent that first summer without me in Dubrovnik on the Adriatic coast. The year was 1935 and I was five years old.

Two of mama's sisters, Mila and Sida, lived in Dubrovnik, with Mila's husband, Gjoko and their children, Zora and Vera. They owned a cafe/restaurant and mother helped to run the restaurant. She must have been quite an asset, as she was a good cook and manager and they asked her to come again the following year for the season. This she did and again proved, apparently, invaluable.

At the end of Summer 1936 to her dismay and disappointment, after thanking her for all her effort and increased sales, aunt Mila and uncle Gjoko said good-bye to my mother and she was back where she started. All she had earned for five months' hard work was her keep. In order to earn this, she told me, she used to get up at 4.30 am, go to the market, then come back and start preparing lunch. During lunch she would act as waitress and cashier. Afterwards, she would help with the washing up, tidy the restaurant, have two hours off and then start on the evening dinners, following the same routine. She would drop into bed, she said, at nearly midnight, tired, but happy that at least she didn't have to worry where the next dinar for food would have to come from.

One very momentous event, which greatly influenced my mother's life and later my own, happened that summer. Aunt Mila and uncle Gjoko had a third daughter, the eldest, Olga, who was even more beautiful than Zora and Vera and was very dainty and delicate, although slightly crippled in one foot and who, three or four years earlier had caught the eye of a good-looking English tourist, Leslie Hammerton, from Sidcup, Kent. Leslie fell in love with Olga and, as he had some knowledge of German and the Medaković family, in common with most Jugoslav citizens also spoke fluent German, after his return to England, he and Olga corresponded. Her written German was not as good as aunt Sida's, so quite often auntie would write love letters to Leslie, while Olga was sunbathing. This shocked my mother who, even before she met him, felt an affinity with Leslie, as she felt they had both been cheated a little in life. Eventually, the year after they met, Leslie and Olga were married in an elaborate Serbian Orthodox ceremony. Uncle Gjoko was of Serbian origin and his children were brought up in the Serbian Orthodox faith.

Two years after their marriage, Leslie and Olga's only son Ivan was born and during the summer of 1936, when my mother was working in Dubrovnik, Leslie, Olga and baby Ivan, then two years old, came to stay with her parents. Leslie and my mother met and fell deeply in love. My mother was 11 years older than Leslie.

At that time and for a year previously, poor Olga had become mentally ill and later was diagnosed with schizophrenia. Leslie was advised that, for the sake of her own and their baby's safety, she ought to be hospitalised, as she could not be left alone, for fear of doing herself harm or setting fire to the house, as she once did.

That year my aunt Marga and uncle Rudi also decided to pay

Dubrovnik a visit, in order that I could see my mother and cousins, as well as my new little English second cousin. We, of course, stayed in the best hotel and I paraded on the beach in my best 'beach pyjamas' which were then the height of fashion. I remember falling down the marble staircase of the hotel, when the Manager came to help me up and then made me very worried, as he showed me a small imperfection in one of the stairs and said that I had damaged the staircase and auntie Marga and uncle Rudi would have to pay for it! Apparently, I immediately stopped crying over my grazed knees.

Not surprisingly, Ivan did not take to me straight away. Being much older - a full four years older - I decided that, as he was my cousin's son, he was the nearest thing to a nephew that I might ever have and insisted that he called me 'auntie' and kissed me. I spoke fluent German and was told that the English language was very similar to German where certain phrases were concerned. "Gib mir ein Kuss!" I kept saying to poor Ivan!

Needless to say he wouldn't kiss me and kept screaming "Go away, go away!" Thus, I learnt my very first two English words and did not learn a single one more until much later, when I was 16.

When my mother arrived back in Zagreb, she found a letter from Leslie asking her to come to England to act as his housekeeper and look after Ivan, for that was the best he could offer. After agonising over her decision, mama decided to go. She discussed her decision with us in Brod and, seeing how happy and contented I was, she went off on her adventure with an easy conscience.

After my mother had been in England for a year, in 1938, she returned to Jugoslavia for the last time before the war, to ascertain again that I was not missing her too much and to have some photographs taken with me. She seemed almost English to me then and I envied her fluency in the language. Little did I realise then that, because she was not so young when she learnt it, her grammar and vocabulary were poor and her accent thick, though to many people in

England she had a very attractive way of speaking. Many years later she told me that she caused much merriment in a shop on one occasion when she demanded a 'bottomful of vinegar' instead of 'a bottleful'.

While I was living in Slavonski Brod with uncle Rudi and auntie Marga, I spent many happy holidays with them in all the popular resorts and spas in Jugoslavia. We often also went skiing in the winter, particularly to Sljeme, a mountain above Zagreb, well known for skiing. Only once did they go by themselves and left me to be looked after by the household staff.

Although I was academically bright, I was a very bad knitter as a child and while I started to knit a sock before aunt and uncle went away for three weeks on the one occasion when they left me, I only managed to knit two rows in that time. As soon as my aunt returned, she finished the complete sock. In our craft lesson in the Junior school, we used to take our work, in turn, to the teacher's desk. That day, I proudly took my sock to the teacher to be inspected and waited for praise. Instead, without lifting her head, the teacher asked: "Has your aunt had an enjoyable holiday?", and I blushed, well aware that she knew who had completed the sock.

Most of the winter afternoons, bearing in mind the fact that school started at 8 am and finished at 1 pm or 2 pm, were spent tobogganing or skiing in a local Park. Although I enjoyed both these sports, particularly skiing, my favourite sport at that time, apart from ping-pong, was sitting on my bottom, usually in my new ski pants, and sliding down the hill. I often used to hear my aunt discussing the fact that my ski pants became torn after less than a week's wear and she had to keep buying me new ones. She presumed, she said, it was because I fell over a lot whilst skiing. I did not bother to enlighten her.

Saints' days and public holidays were very special occasions in towns and villages all over the country, when fairs and stalls would spring up on every available and suitable square or green, and my uncle would take my friends and me whenever he could or had promised.

The most colourful, abundant and popular stalls were 'licitarski' (sweetmeat) stalls, which were hung with the most exciting iced or decorated wares, whose main selling point, in addition to beauty, was the fact that they were edible. The favourite item on these stalls was a 'licitarsko srce', sweetmeat heart. This is so popular and typical of the country, that there is even a national ballet bearing that name. These hearts are usually predominantly red, with elaborate white icing and many tiny inset mirrors, often bearing a motto, and made in different sizes. The biscuit base is quite tasty, a little like gingerbread.

In the evenings of Saints' and market days, even in the smallest villages, there was dancing on the green or in town squares. Each province of Jugoslavia had its own traditions and beautiful national costume, as well as its typical dances which were performed then and which are passed on from generation to generation. I greatly enjoyed researching part of this topic for a thesis on Ritual and Social Drama of the People of Jugoslavia.

Aunt Marga would often write to my mother in England and always enclosed a little letter from me. I would take care to write and tell her what happened at school, what parties I attended and all about the beautiful clothes I was given. On Mother's day, I made her beautiful cards and wrote my own little verses. My mother treasured a particular Mother's Day card that I made for her in 1939, when I was nine; she kept it in her wallet until the day she died, over thirty years later and I found it when I was sorting through her effects!

Although I could never have given a child of mine away, even knowing that I was doing it for her own good, I have forgiven my mother a long time ago for sending me to her brother and sister-in-law. Who knows what internal struggles she conquered or how many tears she shed, wondering whether she was making the right decision and, later, worrying how I was and whether I still even remembered her. Luckily, she had Ivan to bring up and treat as her own and she was much happier with Leslie than she had ever been with my father.

Leslie was a generous man, very intelligent, but when he had a lot to drink, his temper was something we all feared. He also said he could not help being bad-tempered and occasionally drunk, as he was not in the business of selling lemonade, but whisky. He was Export Manager for Hiram Walker, a large, well known whisky firm, who make Canadian Club whisky and travelled abroad quite a lot. It must, therefore, have been a great relief to him to know that mama was looking after his son while he was away.

On one of his travels Leslie visited us in Brod - it must have been in early 1939, I think - and I well remember him saying in German, for none of us could speak English, that my uncle's wine, in fact all Jugoslav wine, was like milk and one could not get drunk on it. He bitterly regretted saying this, for after the Saturday evening's dinner, with wines from our vineyard, I recall him lying in a deckchair in the garden all day Sunday, with a hangover and an ice pack on his head, putting up with a lot of teasing from uncle Rudi! Many memories of those carefree days are still with me: my first satchel, for instance, when I was finally allowed to go to school. Other children slept with dolls or teddy bears, while I slept for weeks with my satchel.

Another memory that I will never forget was the day of my seventh birthday, when I wished for a pair of roller skates and a 'mama' doll with sleeping eyes. I was convinced that this time my wishes would not come true and had almost reconciled myself to the disappointment I would feel, when the day dawned and all I had desired was on the floor beside my bed. I cried with happiness. From that day on I happily roller-skated with a friend called Darija, whenever I had a spare moment. Darija was the daughter of a neighbour and we were close friends, although I knew that her brother, Zeno, was very pro Nazi/fascist, as he wrote some articles on that subject in the local paper, whipping up anti-Jewish feelings.

We were not very religious, as we were Jews who had been christened in the Roman Catholic Church. Thus, we had the best of both worlds, I thought, for was not Jesus born a Jew? I attended all the Jewish celebrations, such as Hanukkah, with my best friend, Fela while, as a family, we celebrated all the Catholic festivals. Of these, St Nicholas' Day, Christmas and Easter were the ones I remember most.

On St Nicholas' day, 6 December, in the evening my uncle would come home from the office and, having hung his coat up in the hall, would come into the lounge to have his pre dinner drink. I would then go through his pockets, with his permission, to find something wrapped in red tissue paper. This was the present St Nicholas supposedly left for me at his office. My favourite present was that which St Nicholas 'delivered' on 6 December 1939, a beautiful red autograph book, all the rage among my school friends, as we were leaving our Junior school at the end of that school year.

Each Christmas Eve we would all go to my Godparents, the Šarić family for pre-Christmas dinner, which was always a very elaborate affair. I loved going to their flat, as it was situated in a tall block on the main square and from their windows one could observe the people promenading down below. As soon as we started our festive dinner, usually consisting of a large carp with side dishes, followed by exquisite desserts, there would be a knock at the door and in would come a few of their neighbours' children about twelve years old, singing traditional Christmas carols and carrying a beautifully constructed home-made cardboard crib, lit from the inside. They would continue singing while we had dinner and, as soon as we had finished eating, we would join in the singing. We would give the children some money and a lot of gold chocolate coins.

All our presents would be under a huge richly decorated Christmas tree in the corner of the room and, as soon as the neighbouring children had departed, we would excitedly open them. I still think it is quite a good idea to open presents in the evening of

Christmas Eve, as Christmas Day is busy enough with cooking, unexpected callers, telephone calls, etc, without the added business of opening presents. It also obviates the need for children to wake their parents up at some ungodly hour, in order to find out what they have been given!

Occasionally, during the evening other groups of children would arrive and we would sing with them, again rewarding them with real and chocolate money. At midnight we would go to a little church for midnight service, then the grown-ups would come back to our house for coffee and more drinks. Everyone lived within short walking distances of each other, so there would be no need for transport.

On Christmas Day we would have lots of people in for drinks in the morning and quite often many of them would stay for lunch and the rest of the day.

Easter was usually spent at the villa in the vineyard, which lent itself perfectly to searching for our Easter eggs left by the Easter Bunny. These we would usually find in beautifully made grass nests fashioned from cut grass. In addition to small and large chocolate eggs, my aunt would dye or paint hard-boiled ones with blue and red colours, or boil eggs in onion skins, which gave them a lovely glossy dark brown colour; I still sometimes do that at Easter for my own children and grandchildren.

As mentioned before, auntie Marga and uncle Rudi usually took me with them wherever they went in the evenings. However, one evening aunt kissed me 'Good night' and was ready to leave when I remonstrated and said that I would like her to stay at home with me. She replied: "What do you think I am, your slave?"

Tearfully I said: "Yes, you are! What is a slave?", which elicited a laughing response, another cuddle and I was, apparently, happy again. This story was oft repeated in company.

If, on occasion, we were not in the vineyard on a Sunday, we would have our lunch, cooked by Jelka, then we would go for a walk to Bosanski Brod, just across the bridge over the river Sava, for the delicious ice cream and Halva, which always tasted better in Bosnia. Both Bosanski Brod and Slavonski Brod suffered terrible damage in the recent insane war and, I believe, the bridge was destroyed. The two towns typified the East and the West.

There are no hot cross buns in ex-Jugoslavia/Croatia, but it is traditional on Good Friday to have a meal with friends, the centrepiece of which was always a huge carp-fish, beautifully displayed and garnished on a large platter, which is similar to that eaten in the evening of Christmas Eve. I can still visualise it over fifty years later.

Unbeknown to me, in September 1939, my mother's new country entered into war with Germany. I did hear about it but, as Jugoslavia was not concerned at that time, the news simply washed over me. Life was still enjoyable. I never lacked anything, although I don't think I was spoiled.

In 1940, while Jugoslavia was still at peace, the day of the biggest challenge of my young life up to then, dawned: the all important day, to which my friends and I looked forward and were preparing for eagerly, the day of that country's equivalent of the 11+ exam. We were so excited, but not at all anxious.

Our examination was completely different from the English 11+, in that it was much more a test of our learnt knowledge than intelligence, although some intelligence questions were contained in the Mathematics paper. We had to complete tests in several subjects, in order to compete for places in the Grammar School (Gymnasium) and, as far as I can remember, these were the subjects: Serbo-Croat, Mathematics, History, Geography, General Science, almost like mini GCSE's. I remember rushing up and down the stairs between each examination, for each one took place in a different room.

Mama and Leslie in their garden in Sidcup

Mama (Elvira) as a young woman, 1925

The proceedings took all day and the results were announced a couple of weeks later. As mentioned before, Zvonko and I were jubilant to find that, although we were the two youngest entrants at just 10 years of age, we tied for the top place. My dream was to come true and I was to attend the Gymnasium, the best and most important school in the town, standing right in the middle of the town square. I was actually to wear the gorgeous uniform worn by other 'big' girls: a navy pleated skirt with a white blouse and navy sailor collar in the summer, to be swapped for a navy blouse with a sailor collar in winter. What joy!

The first thing we had to do when we started the school was to have a passport size photograph taken, to be placed in our student identification card. I carried mine so proudly everywhere, even though my hated freckles showed! I had plaits at the time, having persuaded my aunt that the short bob hairstyle on which she insisted when I was small, was now out of date.

The Gymnasium turned out to be as wonderful as I had expected. New subjects, such as German, were tackled with great enthusiasm and success. Actually, my mother had spoken German to me from the cradle, in order that I would be bilingual from babyhood and, therefore, I found it easy. The German teacher was a very eccentric character and a strict disciplinarian with a dry sense of humour, but he had one pet hate: anyone coughing. He had just finished teaching us the song: "O, du lieber Augustin', which we sung with gusto when, in the silence that ensued, he announced as usual: "Anyone who coughs will be given extra work or detention." He then followed this by the loudest fit of coughing I had ever heard. He had the grace to look embarrassed and left the room, I presume to look for a sip of water! He never again mentioned coughing.

Other subjects, such as Biology and Literature in particular, were my favourite. I revelled in reading poetry, epic stories and books of Jugoslav and foreign authors in translation. At that time, my most read book was Pearl Buck's The Good Earth and I remember feeling very grown up when I was allowed to read it. At the same time, my aunt was reading Emil Zola's Nana, which also interested me, but I was not allowed to read it then.

CHAPTER 3

The War Years (Easter 1941 to May 1945)

My first year at the Gymnasium was almost over, when we woke up one morning in April 1941 and heard that we were at war with Germany, as German troops had entered Jugoslavia via its borders with Austria in Slovenia. We were afraid that we would be flattened by German bombs and hurriedly collected some clothes, food, etc, and made our way by taxi to our villa in the vineyard, where we thought we would be safe. I remember listening to the radio around mid-day, whilst crouching under the table in the enclosed verandah and seeing what I thought was a formation of aeroplanes. We waited for the bombs, which never came. On glancing at the aeroplanes for the second time, we realised that what we saw in reality was a flock of birds! We all dissolved into hysterical laughter with relief.

As everyone now knows, the German/Jugoslav war was a farce, which officially lasted only about a fortnight. Unofficially, however, due to the fierce patriotism and courage of the Partisans and the heroism of the whole of the Jugoslav nation, which refused to be suppressed and oppressed, despite the quislings, the real war against fascism ended at the same time as the war for most of the world, on VE Day, 8 May 1945.

When the fortnight of the so-called bloodless war was up, the Germans had overrun Jugoslavia and helped to install a puppet Government in my part of the country, Croatia, consisting of Ustashe, the anti-royalist, pro-German quislings.

For a little while life was almost normal, though shortages of fruit, such as bananas, became inevitable. Gradually, fewer and fewer people visited us, because it was suspected that we were Jewish and were persona non grata, despite our usual regular visits to our Christian church every Sunday, since our christening. The so called 'loyal' citizens of Slavonski Brod ensured that we, together with many prominent citizens of the town, who were wholly or partly Jewish, were seen nowhere without our shameful and supposedly shaming yellow armband emblazoned with the Star of David.

I could not attend my beloved school any more and, after initial tailing off, my uncle could not go to his office and practise as a barrister, which almost killed him or, at least, killed his self-respect and his wonderful enthusiasm for life and work.

Needless to say, every one of our domestic staff was paid off and gradually, as my aunt's parents, stepbrother and many of our friends disappeared overnight, never to be heard of again, we became a little afraid, although we felt that 'it could never happen to us.'

My uncle did a lot of charity work in his lifetime and often when some poor peasant client he defended had no money, waived his fee. Therefore, he thought that there would be a public outcry if anything happened to him and his family and believed that no one would dare touch us.

All this happened during the remainder of 1941 and the beginning of 1942. Of course, my friend, Fela and her family, together with the rabbi and his family were the first to disappear. However, gradually, despite the loss of my uncle's practice and our house in Brod, we began living permanently and reasonably contentedly in our little modern villa in the vineyard. We had a little money for a while and our neighbours would always pop in with some meat or cabbage or other foodstuffs.

One day, while we were eating our evening meal, my uncle dropped a bombshell. We had nothing more to live on - no money, all his savings had been frozen and the Ustashe had taken all my aunt's jewellery, so we had nothing left to sell or with which to barter. We all cried in despair, but suddenly I had an idea. I knew that our vincilir (caretaker), and the grown up members of his family earned quite a bit of money working in the vineyards and at this time were being paid certain sums of money per hour for carrying manure in baskets on their heads, tipping each basket at the foot of every vine. Therefore, I decided I would ask if I could do this.

I was twelve years old, healthy and strong, while my aunt and uncle were in their late fifties, I think, and getting weaker. Both, in fact, suffered from diabetes and had to give themselves insulin injections two or three times a day. In addition, my aunt suffered from other debilitating illnesses.

At first, my aunt and uncle wouldn't hear of my suggestion, but came to realise it was the only sensible solution to our great problem. However, the biggest objection came from Miloš himself. How could Dr Kolar's niece work with them? It wouldn't feel right! But work with them I did.

On the first day of my first job I woke up very early and reported for work together with all the others. In order to prove that I was worth the money, I tried to work harder than anyone else and carried more baskets per hour than anyone. I overcame my initial reaction of revulsion and retching when I had to fill the first basket with manure, then balance it on my head at the start of the walk towards the first vine. I pretended at first that I was a model learning to walk on the catwalk and was learning poise and deportment. As soon as the first mission was over, I forgot all my reticence and carried on as if I had been born to the work.

It was the proudest moment of my young life when I was paid and gave my aunt and uncle all the money I had earned to buy food and any other necessities. Tears of happiness, as well as sadness greeted me. No money I ever earned during the rest of my life was as precious or as hard earned!

I continued working with all the other workers while there was any nearby vineyard still to be fertilised and was gradually accepted and offered work when there was any available. I still have a scar on my ring finger, which had to be lanced when I sustained an infection during my manure-carrying days! If nothing else, this particular job taught me that all work is honourable and no job is too menial for anybody.

New Year 1943 dawned and we were still living untouched in our vineyard villa. We thought if we lived our lives quietly and never appeared in Brod, but did our shopping at the little village store at the foot of the hills, we would be almost forgotten. Then one night we had some strange visitors. Under the cover of darkness, three figures, who looked like camouflaged soldiers, quietly slipped into the house. Later, I found out that they were partisans who needed shelter and some food and, from that night on, we would frequently provide a stopover for their colleagues. Refreshed, they would rejoin their friends in the forests of Slavonija.

Our new-found friends warned us that our lives and liberty were in danger and advised us to join them. We carefully made our plans. We would tell no one. On the appointed night we would meet two of our friends in a clearing in a small wood nearby and they would lead us to the nearest partisan encampment. Although I was given this information, I was sworn to secrecy and was not even allowed to tell my friend, Seka.

The best laid plans of mice and men oft gang astray.

Two days before we were due to leave to join the partisans and help fight for the freedom of our country, completely unexpectedly, there was a loud knock at the door. It was nearly midnight and we were fast sleep. I presume my uncle opened the door and, after some conversation with the two Ustashe and two German soldiers who stood on the doorstep armed, he invited them in and informed aunt Marga why they were there. The first I knew of their business, apart from the way in which they announced it, was when uncle Rudi came to my bedside and said gently: "Wake up, Verica, they've come for us.

The Ustashe want us to take our personal belongings with us and travel with them by train to Zagreb."

I dressed as quickly as I could, put a few bits of clothing in a small case and remembered to leave a few hairslides in the drawer of my lovely pink bedside cabinet, for when I returned.

We must all have been very naive, even though it was as late as March 1943, to think that we were going on a short journey to Zagreb, a journey which we had often made before on business or for pleasure, for some questioning and that we would then return to resume our simple everyday lives. How wrong we were!

It is very rarely in man's interest to know what lays in store for him. I am sure very few people would be courageous enough ever if they knew in advance what awaits them in the future. I was just thirteen years old when we left our home in the vineyards.

When we came off the train in Zagreb, we were shepherded, like criminals, into a Black Maria, which delivered us at the gates of the large, infamous prison on Savska Cesta. Everyone knew the prison, as it was in the past, before the war, used purely for criminals, but now it had a more sinister use as the collection point for consignments to concentration camps in Germany, mainly Auschwitz.

On arrival, we were not questioned, as expected, but were placed in a very large room on the first floor, with about sixty other people. The door, of course, was locked.

We were to spend two weeks in that room in close proximity, sleeping on our coats on the wooden floor. There was only one toilet with a tiny wash-basin in a small corridor off the large room, which was always in demand, of course.

I am very sorry that I did not pay much attention to the other occupants of that room, for I am sure they were all extremely interesting, intelligent and good people, undeserving of the fate in store for them. All I remember, apart from a middle aged regal looking Japanese lady, who taught me a little Japanese rhyme, was the fact that I was by far the youngest person in there. The following is the rhyme which is indelibly etched on my mind:

Oto mano mano saki
Sazo yeno tsubayaki,
Nante mango, inge so!

To this day I remember her and her rhyme, but have never managed to find out what it means. This lady could also read palms and was apparently excellent at telling everyone his or her character and events from their past, though I don't remember her forecasting anyone's future. When I asked her to read my palms, she shook her head and gently said, without looking at them: "I'm sorry, my dear, but you are too young. Not enough has happened in your young life for me to say much."

After two weeks in this room, the warders came to collect us and told us that we were being moved to another part of the prison, as the large room was needed for other people. We were then separated into males and females, placed in separate cells and our prison life really started in earnest.

There were 26 females, who were placed in two cells. Our cell, about 12 ft by 9 ft, accommodated the thirteen of us on its cement floor. The only light was natural light, which came through the bars of a small, high window on the outside wall. No more visits to the toilet. All we needed was the bucket, which stood in the corner and reminded us of our frail humanity. This was emptied by two of us twice a day: early morning and early evening. I was usually one of the two carriers as, unlike most of them, I was young, strong and healthy.

Two other privileges were afforded us whilst we were in this cell: a daily walk around the prison yard in twos, for twenty minutes, no talking permitted and a weekly cold shower. One can imagine the trepidation with which I awaited the weekly shower - a shy, thirteen year old, naked, with so many other women of all ages, most of them married and much older.

The food in prison was very frugal, mostly bread and soup, I think. One day was like another in our cell and we soon forgot what date it was. I knew that soon on 13 June would be the feast of St Anthony and, therefore, I prayed most fervently to that saint to intercede with God on our, or was it my (?), behalf, for God to be so gracious as to grant us freedom again and deliver us from this hardship. Even then I could not be sure what the dates were, but I reasoned that neither God nor the Saint would mind my being early or late with my prayers. In any case, every night and morning and often in between, I would pray Our Father, Hail Mary, numerous times and, my favourite, Hail, Queen, Mother of God, which I had only recently learnt.

The first week in the cell passed reasonably quickly. However, after that our backs and bodies began hurting from sleeping on damp concrete. Whichever way we moved, we ached and by the end of the second week most of us suffered severe headaches and felt dizzy.

We had no books, no paper, no craft equipment; in fact, nothing, except the clothes on our backs and the bucket in the corner.

Although I always feel sorry nowadays when I read about the deprivation and overcrowding in our prisons, full of criminals and lawbreakers, I often think of the deprivation and overcrowding suffered by us, the innocent victims of a madman and his band of helpers. We just had our own personalities and resources, in order to sustain each other when we reached rock bottom, or help to keep each other's spirits up by prayer and singing or story telling. There were many religions represented in our throng, including Shinto, Jewish, Moslem, Serbian Orthodox and Roman Catholic. None of us knew why we were there, although I presume many, like my family, were there because they were thought to be Jewish and had helped the partisans or were planning to join these fighters for freedom.

After three weeks in our separate cells, we were all again reunited for a day or two in the large room on the first floor. We thought it was because we would soon be released. Somehow rumours were rife in that room, though their sources were always obscure. Perhaps some kind guard, in return for favours rendered (we all knew though did not discuss what these were - a gold watch here, a couple of hours of passion there), would whisper what most of us wanted to hear.

Some time towards the end of May, I think, the room was unlocked, one of the warders entered and asked: "Which one of you is Verica Šlezinger?" When I went forward and said that I was that person, he added: "You are to come with me."

I kissed my aunt and uncle quickly, grabbed my coat and bag and went with the warder. Very briefly, my uncle said: "Perhaps you are going to be released" but, although the thought had also struck me, I discounted it. What was so special about me? Nothing, except had I not implored St Anthony, my special Saint, that I might find freedom and was he not especially concerned with finding lost things?

However, I said 'Au revoir' or, rather, 'Do vidjenja', the Croatian equivalent, to aunt and uncle and really believed that, after some query was cleared up in the office of the prison, I would rejoin them. But that was the last time I saw them alive and to this day have not heard definitely what happened to them. It is all too easy to conjecture on their fate or that of all those who were in that room with me in the spring of 1943. However, I know that they were sent to Auschwitz and never returned. In any case, both suffered ill health and had their spirit broken. Even if they were not killed, they could not have survived. I only hope that they were aware of the fact that I was free and, because of their great love for me, this was of some consolation.

When the warder took me downstairs, I was received by a uniformed man, who introduced me to a gentleman standing nearby and asked me matter of factly: "Miss Šlezinger, do you know this gentleman?"

Something inside me told me to say: "Yes", though I had never seen him. To this, the first man said: "Good!", and sent me with the warder to be fingerprinted and photographed full and side face, as is customary with criminals. As soon as this was done, I was asked to sign a form and was formally handed over to the gentleman, who witnessed these proceedings. He took me by the hand and we walked out of the prison into the twilight of a warm day.

When we had been clear of the prison, whilst I was uncertain of the mixture of my emotions: disbelief, shock, relief and terror, the gentleman, who turned out to be a Dr M, a friend of my father's, said: "Don't be too nervous, Verica, your daddy is waiting around the corner."

For this I was totally unprepared! To be free at last, so unexpectedly quickly would have been enough, but to be reunited with my father as well! The joy that I felt was indescribable. I ran towards the corner and felt unbelievable love and relief to be cradled in my father's arms. He, too, apparently never believed that this moment would come and only later did I realise what it had cost him, not financially, I believe, but in other ways. He could just murmur: Dušo, dušo (darling, darling)! After a moment and without further explanations, we walked on, too full of emotion to speak much. However, I asked where we were going and was told that a condition of my release was that I would live at the Orphanage of St Anthony (Antunovac), in order to be re-educated.

In charge of the orphanage was the order of nuns called Sisters of Little Jesus and they were to be in charge of me until VE Day. The orphanage was to be my home, for better or worse until then.

That first evening I was taken to Antunovac, introduced to Sisters Mary Gaudencija and Mary Asumpta and met all the children, who varied in ages from two to sixteen or seventeen. Tata told me he would come to see me the following day and explain everything. I was satisfied with that and, although I was sorry to part from him so soon, I quickly got into the bed, which I was shown was mine, in the senior dormitory.

After a prayer of thanksgiving and one that I would soon be reunited with my aunt and uncle, outside the prison, of course, I fell into an exhausted sleep, surrounded by bedsful of chattering children, eager to make the acquaintance of the newcomer.

Exactly at the promised time next day, my father came to take me out to auntie Jelka and uncle Emil for the day and to offer me an explanation for my good fortune. And it was unbelievable good fortune for me, for my aunt Marga and uncle Rudi, together with all the other people whose lives we shared in that prison for about two months, were despatched by train from Zagreb to Auschwitz concentration camp the next day for extermination and were never heard of again.

The best proof I had of this was my literally shocking and unexpected discovery in the Mormon Genealogical Library in Salt Lake City in March 2001 of a consignment note of 25 female prisoners received in that camp on 23 May from Zagreb, the day after Dr M rescued me. That was the number of female inmates left after I walked out of the prison. I was not looking for it, merely trying to establish, if I could, in that thoroughly researched and documented building, what had happened to some of my schoolfriends and my aunt and uncle. Even now, three years after the event, I still feel the tingling in my spine, the head-spinning mixed thoughts and feelings that resulted from my awesome discovery. The poems which follow had to be written, in order to expiate my probably needless guilt at being here, so many years later, to tell the tale.

Even today, despite the impossibility of recognition, due to the state of the inmates, I always make myself watch all concentration camp films on television or in the cinema, just in case I can see my aunt and uncle. I tried to acccess the Auschwitz website several times, but it always seems down. Graham has promised me that we would try to visit the camp next year, if I can bear it.

It was accepted in Zagreb that everyone from our consignment, except for me, had perished. The only person from Slavonski Brod who might have survived, I heard, was my aunt's stepbrother, Fritz, who disappeared several months before our arrest, but no one in Brod knows that for certain.

There is a thick book, Holocaust in Zagreb, which I have bought, but it contains several inaccuracies, including the wrong date for my father's death. Nevertheless, it charts a part of my family's and my history and is, therefore, of value to me.

Date	Origin	Total	F	M	Notes
[...]					
7.5.1943	RSHA Gh Saloniki	1000	68	—	c,h
7.5.1943	Posen	45	45	—	a
7.5.1943	Sammeltransport	198	66	132	a
7.5.1943	RSHA Zagreb	1000	—	40	c,h
7.5.1943	Deutschland	17	—	17	a
8.5.1943	geboren	1	—	1	d
8.5.1943	geboren	3	2	1	n
8.5.1943	Sammeltransport	84	—	84	a
8.5.1943	Krakau	33	9	24	a
8.5.1943	Kattowitz	11	—	11	a
8.5.1943	Oppeln	1	—	1	a
8.5.1943	RSHA Gh Saloniki	2500	247	568	h
9.5.1943	Deutschland	12	4	8	a
9.5.1943	KL Buchenwald	2	—	2	a
9.5.1943	Kattowitz	2	2	—	a
10.5.1943	geboren	2	—	2	n
10.5.1943	Deutschland	32	14	18	a
10.5.1943	Sammeltransport	24	8	16	a
11.5.1943	Sammeltransport	9	9	—	a
11.5.1943	Kattowitz	19	—	19	a
11.5.1943	Oppeln	1	—	1	a
11.5.1943	Krakau	38	6	32	a
11.5.1943	Posen	43	5	38	a
12.5.1943	Bialystok	971	503	468	a
12.5.1943	Österreich	76	31	45	a
12.5.1943	Kattowitz	9	2	7	a
12.5.1943	Krakau	35	10	25	a
13.5.1943	geboren	1	1	—	d
13.5.1943	geboren	1	1	—	n
13.5.1943	Krakau	6	6	—	a
13.5.1943	Sammeltransport	17	17	—	a
13.5.1943	Kattowitz	10	—	10	a
13.5.1943	Koblenz	1	—	1	a
13.5.1943	Warschau	456	119	337	a
13.5.1943	RSHA Zagreb	1000	25	30	c,h
14.5.1943	Krakau	29	—	29	a
14.5.1943	Sammeltransport	99	—	99	a
					[...]

"The Find" in the Genealogical Museum in Salt Lake City
- copy of the records of consignments to Auschwitz, May 1943

THE FIND

Although faint in substance
it still seems etched in memory
like the imprint of a leaf
with veins proud on its reverse,

the silence of the night
broken by breathing,
some shallow and fast
like a baby's,
other laboured;

yet more quite noisy
with accompanied snores,
making one wait
for the next onslought.

Twenty-six females in all:
thirteen to each cell,
camping on damp concrete,

each wall as damp
as our frightened breath -
how long we'll stay together,
how long before death?

A lowly bucket in the corner
to see to our bodily waste,
a walk in the yard each day,
for one hour
precisely.

Once a week we shower
naked, together;
there is no shame
we're all the same.

The Japanese lady takes pity,
She says she's old and I'm only 13;
I feel as old as Methuselah.

She teaches me a Japanese song
which I'll never forget,
yet still don't know what it means.

Days turn into weeks,
weeks into months.
I pray, constantly:

St Anthony, please rescue me!
Holy Mary, Queen of Sinners,
take pity!
I'm too young to die.
Jesus, Son of God,
save me
and all in here!
Adonai, we trust in you!

At last, someone
has heard my prayer
and come.

I'm photographed
like a criminal,
my fingerprints are saved
for posterity
and I'm free;

almost free to roam,
but kept in a home
for orphans
of St Anthony!

All memories locked away
where they'll always stay!

Until, in Salt Lake City
in March 2001, I find
the consignment note
of female prisoners
received in Auschwitz
from Zagreb, in May '43:
Twenty five in all.

In the momentary comfort and safety of aunt Jelka's and uncle Emil's home, my father told me that when he managed to discover that I was imprisoned on Savska Cesta, by bribing several people, he had one of his hare-brained schemes. Unlike most of those in the past, this one actually worked and I owe my life to it, as well as to his very kind and exceptional friends, Dr and Mrs M, who agreed to be part of the plan.

My father conceived the idea of asking Dr M to state in an affidavit that I was his illegal daughter, the product of a clandestine relationship between himself and my mother, the year before I was born. This, of course, could not have worked if my mother had been living in Zagreb at the time, because it would have been impossible for her to accept this slur on her good name. In truth, she had never even met the man, but he demanded my release on the basis of the fact that, as his daughter, I had every right to be at liberty and not incarcerated.

When my father had finished telling me the story of my release, aunt Jelka suggested I had a bath, for which suggestion I was grateful. However, in the bath I realised with horror that I had body lice, as well as those that lived in my hair. My relations, therefore, obtained permission for me to stay there for two or three days, until these could be eliminated. All my clothes had to be burnt and aunt asked her friends for clothes for me.

I often had hair lice in the orphanage, in common with other children there and we were frequently checked. However, never did I feel as bad or as unclean as on that day. Every time I hear someone these days say that he/she is feeling 'lousy', I am tempted to regale him/her with my story when I was feeling and had really been literally lousy, but so far have always resisted the temptation.

When I returned to the orphanage, my father visited me every evening and made friends with Sister M Assumpta, who was very young, very sweet, kind and my favourite. I realised what a wonderful person my father was, too, and what a good sense of humour he had, despite his bad asthma, thrombosis and general ill health caused by his participation in the First World War.

Our reunion and joy in each other's company after so many years of deprivation, was short lived. Exactly three weeks to the day of my release, my father was arrested. I never managed to find out if his arrest was the direct result of my release or was made in connection with some other matter, but he was dead within a week. That much I know to be true, although whether he was shot in prison, as rumoured, or whether he died due to his bad health and lack of medication, I shall never know for certain. What questions the Second World War, more than any other war, left unanswered!

NAKED DIVERSITY

Often, when I undress
ready for a bath or shower
my mind returns
to the weekly showers
I took with other females
in Savska Cesta,
when I was thirteen

reluctant to take my clothes off
be naked in front of others.
My body was developing
I began to have breasts
though very small.
Other ladies were older,
some very old,
their breasts pendulous;
I hoped mine would never
become like that -
now they have,
but I'm still here
my companions all perished.

How I longed for a bath
to immerse my whole body
in deep water!
To relax and lose myself,
dissolving all cares
acquired by sleeping
on damp concrete.
To wash away the smells
which permeated us all
after using the bucket
in the corner of our cell.

How lucky I am now!
I can anticipate entering the bath
whenever I wish,
unseen by prying eyes;
the only eyes, apart from mine,
my darling husband's.
After a lifetime together
if he enters the bathroom
embraces me, it is soothing,
taking away all the memories
of those other preparations.

Keeping busy
(First on the left next to the nun)

Group photograph at the orphanage
(I'm first on the left, second row standing)

Sisters M Carmelita and M Gaudencija were in charge of the Junior and Senior children at the orphanage, but it was in my talks with Sister M Asumpta that I sought solace after the loss of my father. Because she knew him, she seemed to understand my loss better and I am sure his death would have affected me much more and I would not have been able to get over it permanently, if it had not been for her. She grieved with me, thus helping me to reconcile myself with another blow dealt by fate.

Each Sunday I would go to auntie Jelka and uncle Emil. I appreciated the walk from the orphanage through their avenue of mature trees to their sunny flat. We would talk freely and I would feel part of a family again. Auntie Jelka was, after all, my father's favourite sister. Although she was pleased to see me, this was a very sad time for her. When her parents sold their village shop in Kozice they, together with Jelka's unmarried sister, Thea, came to live with her and Emil. My father's brother, Karl, also lived in Zagreb and often visited them, until he, too, disappeared. I remember him as a very dashing and popular young man, much younger than my father.

Within a very short space of time, my grandmother had died and my grandfather, auntie Thea and uncle Karl were imprisoned and sent to concentration camps never to be heard of again. Also, my two other aunts, Elsa and Olga and their husbands, father's sisters and brothers-in-law, together with their children, were arrested, with the same end result. The loss of my cousins Herta and Elsa, Olga's daughters, particularly saddened me. The only other brother of my father who was then still alive, had emigrated years before and lived in Detroit, Michigan and, although I believe him to be dead now, I have cousins still living there, but have never met any of them. God willing, I hope I will have time some day to trace them.

As well as visiting auntie Jelka and uncle Emil on some Sundays, I began on alternate Sundays to visit another auntie Marga, who was a cousin of the aunt Marga from Slavonski Brod. I used to know her from her occasional visits to us in Brod, before the war and we suddenly met in the street one day. I loved going to her large, beautifully furnished, opulent flat, which was always full of interesting people. She was an excellent and popular hostess, as well as a beautiful and intelligent middle-aged woman, who seemed to be always surrounded by an aura of mystique, which fascinated men, attracting them like a magnet.

Another coincidence - synchronicity - happened to me at that time. We were occasionally sent by Mother Superior at the orphanage to run errands into town and I would often volunteer to go. Perhaps it was something to do with the fact that I could not bear to be cooped up. On one of these errands, when I had volunteered to deliver something to one of our benefactors, I felt a little lighter in heart than usual. I walked through the town among happy, busy people, where I lost myself and was part of the normal world, where people led ordinary, everyday lives.

As I walked up the seemingly endless spiral staircase in the imposing old building to the address given to me, I had a fleeting feeling that something good, for a change, was about to happen to me, though I knew not why. Perhaps the lady of the house will invite me in and offer me a biscuit or a piece of home made cake and a cup of hot chocolate or a glass of orange squash. I might even be allowed to sit in the lounge in a comfortable armchair, reminiscent of my home in Brod. However, never in my wildest dreams was I prepared for the coincidence, which was about to happen. Still day-dreaming, I rang the bell.

After a brief pause, the door was opened by a maid who ushered me into the kitchen, where a lady was busy cooking chicken Maryland, with just chicken legs. To my delight, the lady offered me cakes and a drink, though I cannot remember what the drink was. It was probably coffee. Delighted, after making a polite attempt at refusal, I accepted. This was an art: too hearty a refusal might have been accepted and I would have cried about it all the afternoon; too eager an acceptance might have been interpreted as rudeness or greed.

During the conversation, the lady asked me my name and, when I told her, she said that years ago she had a best friend with whom she lost touch, who was called Elvira Šlezinger. She asked if Elvira could possibly be a distant relative of mine, although it was quite a common name. When I told her that it was my mother, she kissed and hugged me and said I must come often to see her and she would write to Sister M Gaudencija to this effect. Needless to say, she asked me to stay to lunch and I nearly accepted. The thought of having these succulent chicken legs warmed my spirit, but luckily I found out in time that they were really that rare delicacy beloved in France, frogs' legs and I managed to refuse gracefully by saying that I was expected for lunch at Antunovac. However, my newfound aunt invited me round again soon. On one of my later visits she discovered that I had not yet been confirmed and arranged for my confirmation to take place in the not too distant future. She had a beautiful dress made for me out of some antique white lace and, as my Godmother, gave me a gold necklace with a pendant of Virgin Mary cradling the infant Jesus in her arms, which I have passed recently to a friend's baby on her christening.

We had a wonderful day for my confirmation, when I was about fourteen and a half and had many photographs taken. In conversation on that day I discovered that my benefactress' husband was the doctor who had performed my mother's abortion before I was born!

Life at the orphanage was very uneventful, particularly for me, because during the first year there I was not allowed to go to school. I had now not attended school for over two years and, although I read all the books I could get, I was eager to learn and felt the injustice of being deprived of the opportunity, when the most important and most loved part of my life had been school, from the moment I began my schooling. Eventually, after more than a year, I was allowed to join a class at the Sisters of Mercy Gymnasium in the centre of the town. It was wonderful to be back at school, working, absorbing knowledge and competing on an equal footing with others of similar abilities, after stagnating for so many months, although I was not allowed to be registered and, therefore, could not have reports, like the others. I presume the fact of my non-registration was for my own protection, but I'm not sure.

Although life was pretty humdrum, it did have some excitement occasionally; at least, some events seemed important and exciting to me. For instance, the nuns were very friendly with the German officers and soldiers who were billeted in a nearby school building. It seemed natural, therefore, for them to use me as a go-between, to invite the officers to dinner. I did not feel any resentment at those times, curiously enough, but felt important to be chosen, because I could speak German. I find this hard to understand now but, I suppose, children quickly forget any injustice and like to feel helpful and especially picked for attention. I have recently heard that well after the end of the war most of the nuns were defrocked, Antunovac was closed and at least two of the nuns, one of them Sister M Gaudencija, were shot as traitors.

The only time the elaborate dinner given by the nuns rankled was when we girls were desperately hungry and occasionally 'borrowed' the keys to the food cupboard to steal some bread. We were all thin and undernourished most of the time and after the war I remember being taken to the doctor at the local hospital by auntie Marga, to be seen by a friend of my father's, in order to investigate the result of this starvation. The true effect of my prison and orphanage days did not manifest itself until many years later, when I was in my late twenties and thirties. At that time it manifested itself merely in the loss of my periods. I had started menstruating while we lived in the vineyard and had been as regular as clockwork for a few months, but from the moment we arrived at Savska Cesta and almost throughout my days in the orphanage, I had had no periods and was worried that perhaps I could not have children later on.

However, a few months after the war ended and I was privileged enough to eat decent food and had good care, as the doctor predicted, all returned too normal.

Another important event was the day the governors of Antunovac were going to pay us a visit. We all had our duties that we had to fulfil every day. Some of us had to clean the dormitory, some had to help old Sister M Ursula in the kitchen, yet others had to sweep the yard or help in the Knitting Department. In addition to running the orphanage, the Sisters had a Machine Knitting Department, which made garments for sale. For the governors' visit we all had new dresses issued, we swept the yard till it was clean enough for their dirty shoes. We were carefully positioned, in order to be seen clean and happy amid antiseptic surroundings.

There was one room in the orphanage to which I retreated at regular intervals, in addition to the times when we were all expected to be there: the beautiful chapel, where the well educated old priest reigned supreme. There, in the quietude, I communicated in oft spoken prayers with God. Not necessarily the God of the Catholic Church or the Adonai of the Jews or even the God of any other religion, but the supreme being, our Father, who hears our prayers, who is Almighty and benevolent. I figured, despite all the unhappiness in the world, there must be an Almighty being who was responsible for our creation, who loves us, because He is capable of invoking such fervent prayers and be capable of producing such beauty in nature and because he has made us capable of such tender feelings of love, such as a mother's towards her baby. After many months, I was chosen to serve at Mass every morning at 5 am or 6 am for a week and was very proud to do so.

I often found solace in writing poetry and still do but, although I thought that I wrote verses on many subjects, most of my poems at that time were addressed and dedicated to and about my mother. I suppose every daughter, particularly if she has been parted from her mother, idealises and idolises her.

INSPECTION

Today is an important
day of inspection;
higher authorities are coming
to inspect the orphanage
and us.

The dormitory must be clean,
The forecourt must be swept
of leaves; people must sit tidily,
appear busy, happy to be there
in unfamiliar clothes
especially procured
for today.

Never mind that we're hungry,
we're also eager to please.
Maybe Sister Ursula
will rustle up enough
for us all to eat tonight,
or maybe we'll get
some extra bread
instead.

I was asked to go
to the German officers
billeted at the school next door
to invite them to dinner
tomorrow night.
I knew my German
would come in useful
some day!

CHAPTER 4
The Post War Period

We were so cocooned in our every day mundane world, bombarded with German propaganda, that we did not realise that the end of the European part of World War II was imminent. Suddenly, without any warning, the war had ended and I was technically free to go where I pleased. But where and to whom should I go?

There was no one left in Slavonski Brod with whom I could stay and pick up the threads of my life. Although technically an orphan - I never knew my mother's address in England, as auntie Marga had always addressed our letters to her and for all I knew my mother was probably dead - I was lucky in that here in Zagreb there were two homes and two family units which wanted me. Although auntie Jelka and uncle Emil were very upset that I did not choose them, in view of later developments, it was providential that I did not.

I chose to leave the Antunovac orphanage for the loving home of auntie Marga No 2, the cousin of my original aunt of that name. She was a widow, whose only son, a nineteen-year-old handsome youth, was one of the first to be taken away from Zagreb and never heard of again. Therefore, auntie Marga said I seemed to have been sent from heaven, someone for her to cherish and love. The only other member of her household in that spacious flat was an elderly lady, who used to be her maid 'in the good old days'. She did the housework in return for bed, board and pocket money, but she was always treated like an elderly relative.

The next few months following VE Day were gloriously happy, eventful and crowded with wonderful memories, events and experiences. After so many months of virtually barely existing a sort of half-life, where melancholy thoughts and the feeling of hunger preoccupied my mind, at the age of fifteen I began to live the life of a real teenager.

The celebrations started on VE Day, when the main square in Zagreb, now named Trg Bana Jelačića again, but a few months after the end of the war was known as the Square of the Republic, was full of happy, singing and dancing people of all ages. However much I am proud to be British now and very anglicised, the sound of Slavonic folk music and dancing never fails to touch my heart. That night, the music, camaraderie, happiness and dancing in the square touched the hearts of many. There was laughter and joy which knew no bounds, but there were also tears, shed and unshed, for those we knew and had lost and for those presumed dead, but still nurtured hope that they would somehow return from the unknown. We knew that even if they did not return, they would live forever in our hearts and that our memories would ennoble them and keep their spirit alive. Songs would be composed glorifying their names and their bravery.

The singing and dancing in the square took place every evening for many days, always starting spontaneously with a few young people and then developing into a mass of round 'kolos',* until they encompassed the whole square. I should imagine the English street parties and the atmosphere in London on VE day were similar.

Until the end of the war I did not realise the extent and size of the glorious partisan army, under the able and visionary leadership of the man the world was to admire for his humanity and his special brand of Communism, which singled Jugoslavia later as a fair and friendly land, Josip Broz TITO. I am sure that if Tito had been alive in the nineties, the bloody war, which has ruined the country, killed so many innocent people and left thousands homeless in refugee camps and wandering the world, would never have happened.

I cannot remember much else about that summer, the summer of 1945, except that it passed very quickly and that I was happy for the first time for many years, yet so much was happening. I was bought

---

* *kolo - dance in the round*

my first bra, went to my first dance, my first teenage party where I had my first proper kiss from a young man by the name of Stanko Skorczinsky. He was about 22, I think, and asked if he could kiss me. I remember replying that I didn't know how to kiss, which didn't seem to deter him! I never saw him again, but his name has stayed with me all these years, so it must have been a pleasant and memorable experience!

Most citizens of Zagreb who were not traitors, particularly the younger element, congregated once a week in community rooms set aside in every street, much like the Community Association premises in our town Harlow, in England, in order to express joy in liberation and hope for the future of our beloved country. We would hold weekly meetings, at which we would read poems by famous poets, sang songs or read our own compositions. We also had what was called a Wall Magazine, a large piece of cardboard the length of a wall, about 4 ft wide, on which the Editor stuck or pinned contributions. Many of my own poems appeared on that wall. At this time the subject of my poetry changed from Mother and Melancholy Thoughts to Tito, To Be Free, My Beloved Country and others in a similar vein.

The president of our small Community Association was Professor Rudolf Filipović, who was Professor of English Literature at Zagreb University. Many years later, when I was researching material for a thesis on English Social Drama for my Certificate in Education, at Senate House in London, I came across some books written by him on the comparison of the work of a well-known Croatian poet with Shakespeare's work. Still later, I heard that he had married a good friend of my best friend Andy and his wife.

As it became high summer, I began wondering what school I would attend in the future. I had only had a few months' schooling at the Convent school and had missed so much, when I saw an article in the local newspaper, advising the citizens of Zagreb that in September 1945 a Partisan Gymnasium would open, in order that the young people who were members of the partisan forces during the war and had been unable to attend school, would be educated. In the special school, because of the different ages and different requirements, according to the number of years of schooling lost, two normal years in a grammar school would be telescoped into one. Because of their maturity, it was expected that the pupils would be more than able to cope with the pressure of work. As an afterthought, at the end of the article, it was stated that the Partisan Gymnasium would also accept pupils who had lost education through imprisonment or victimisation.

The day of enrolment in September 1945 arrived. I was one of the first in the queue and was accepted to study years 3 and 4 during the next scholastic year. I was happy at last and, once the school term had started, almost ecstatic.

The school was run more on the lines of a Technical College than a school and the pupils were treated as mature students which, in fact, we all were, whatever our age. The teachers, lecturers really, whom we called 'drug' or 'drugarica' (comrade - male or female), were picked for their excellence. We revelled in the knowledge acquired daily and no pressures were too great. The friendships which developed in our class and, I presume, others also, were beyond compare. We shared our experiences, our hopes for the future, our ambitions. There were girls, such as Judita Seke, who had returned outwardly unscathed from concentration camps, except for the number tattooed on the inside of their arms. There were boys of 18, such as Ivan Pirker, who had seen battles and taken part in partisan ambushes, whose young faces belied their maturity, forged in the thick forests of Bosnia. His ambition at the time, I remember, was to work for the Ambulance Service and I heard later he was head of it eventually in Zagreb!

One such sixteen-year-old boy, nearly a year older than me, became my best friend and our friendship has now lasted for almost sixty years. Until recently, he was a consultant paediatrician at Toronto Sick Children's Hospital and a few years ago Graham, our daughter, Tanja and I were lucky enough to spend a week staying with him and his charming wife. When we met again after many years, it was just as if we had been together the week before. Real friendships are like that and I feel I have been lucky in my friends, because sometimes there is a gap of several years, even fifteen or more, and then we meet and do not feel strange or awkward at all, just resume our warm friendships. The family of Andy and Tonica, his wife, are like that and both our families are great friends now. They have two sons and I can see the young Andy in his eldest son, Marko, who is also a doctor in Toronto.

Andy was the son of a Jugoslav Doctor and his American born wife and my friendship with him uncovered another great synchronicity. Apparently, years ago, long before my mother married, Andy's father was her family doctor!

My female best friend at that time was Renata Hanapel, another girl like me, who had very few relations left. In her case, she only had grandparents and knew what it was to be deprived of parents at an early age. We used to go dancing together and at one of these dances I met a very likeable young man called Gido Kraus. I still liked Andy very much, but he obviously only wanted a platonic friendship at that time and I suppose I wanted romantic love, holding hands, etc. Although Andy and I walked around for miles and talked much, sometimes sitting in cafes for hours sipping coffee, it was to Gido that I attached my fantasies. We had been dancing together twice a week for a couple of months, when Gido dropped a bombshell: his family was leaving for Israel and we would never see each other again. I thought I would be upset by this piece of news, but I was not; I just transferred all my love to Andy, despite the fact that he was not interested in me as a girl, just as a best friend.

I must have been a typical, very romantic teenage girl after all at that time, living up in the clouds, for I remember, during a chemistry lesson, writing a particularly serious poem about a lighthouse beacon swathed in swirling fog, whilst the Chemistry teacher was illustrating the spontaneous combustion of phosphorus in air, by placing a piece of phosphorus in a spoon in a glass jar. I dare say, I did it especially to impress Andy, who was sitting next to me.

It is at this point that I ought to return to the subject of my mother. When England entered the war in 1939, she reconciled herself to the fact that, for the duration of the war, she would be unable to write to us or receive any mail from Jugoslavia. Although she was very intelligent and well read, she apparently stopped reading newspapers when the war begun and did not read them again until it had finished. This seems almost unbelievable to me, yet it was true. She, therefore, had no idea at all what had happened in Jugoslavia, knew nothing about the German invasion and oppression, about concentration camps, etc. When, after we were reunited I queried how it could possibly be that she did not read the papers throughout this period, she retorted with absolute conviction: "God didn't want me to worry. He wanted to spare me the horror stories of events in Europe. Obviously, had I known what was happening to you, I would not have survived and you need me now, so I had to survive!" She was right, of course.

One night in 1944, Ivan told me, a V1 bomb dropped on a First Aid Dispersion Station in Willersley Avenue, Sidcup. The blast made their home at 130 Willersley Avenue uninhabitable. At the time of the blast, mama, Ivan and Leslie's sister, Connie, were inside the Morrison shelter and Ivan became quite nervous and traumatised as a result. In the morning Connie took him for a while to her Auntie Vi's house in Ilford, while some arrangements could be made for him and mama to be evacuated to a perceived safer place. As Leslie's father had owned a sweet shop years before in Somerset in Weston-Super-Mare, it was decided that they should go there.

Ivan describes Mrs Marshall's boarding house where he and mama stayed as 'interesting' and I remember mama calling it quaint or funny peculiar. There was no electricity, just gaslights, which gave a surprisingly pink, soft light. At night-time, they used to go up to bed carrying their candles and chamber-pots, Ivan recollects.

Although after five or six months he went to school, for many weeks Ivan enjoyed the freedom of running wild along the beach and playing with other children who were in the same boat. He remembers going to the Saturday morning pictures for the price of 6d with his girlfriend of the same age (about nine), who lived in a nearby hotel with her parents. His pocket money, which he received monthly in the form of a five shillings postal order, would go far.

Meanwhile, Leslie joined the 14th Army and was sent to Burma. Post, apparently, took a long time to be exchanged and if Ivan or mama wrote to him, it was a long while before they could expect an answer.

During her time in Weston-Super-Mare, mama said she longed to be back home, so that she could cook the good and varied food, which she always prepared for her family. When she eventually returned with Ivan to Sidcup, she took up the threads of her life. She wrote a long letter to auntie Marga, uncle Rudi and me in Slavonski Brod, telling us of the hardship and evacuation she endured during the war and waited eagerly for our reply, expecting it to contain news of uncle's continuing prosperity and photographs of the teenage young lady into which she confidently expected me to have developed.

When mama's letter was returned with the remarks 'Unknown at this address - Return to Sender', she wrote a couple more letters and still equally confidently expected replies. However, when these, too, were returned in a similar manner, she began to worry.

At this time, my mother had a cleaning lady, a Mrs Alloway, who was a keen spiritualist, and often talked to mama about this subject. Although mother did not take her seriously, one day when Mrs A suggested that mama should accompany her to a spiritualist meeting that afternoon, mama had ran out of excuses and agreed, just for a laugh she thought, as she had nothing better to do that day.

On the way to the meeting, Mrs A advised my mother not to be too disappointed if the medium had no message for her, as usually it was many weeks before there were messages for newcomers. My mother was, therefore, totally unprepared for the surprise of that afternoon. She kept silent at the beginning, in case the medium discovered that she had a foreign accent and used this information in the perpretation of the fraud, which my mother at that time believed spiritualism to be.

As soon as the séance had begun, the medium walked over to my mother and said: "I have some people here, so many of them, they're so excitable and they're all talking at once in a funny, foreign language. Do you understand?"

My mother nodded, as she didn't know what to say.

The medium kept repeating: "Wait a minute. I must get my guide to interpret."

She then turned to my mother again. "I have your mother here and she said that she is pleased you have found happiness at last. I also have your husband here."

To that my mother replied: "You can't have. He is not dead."

"But he says he is," said the medium. "He says that he and most of your relatives are dead, but your daughter is alive and well and you will receive a letter from her soon. He also says that he would like to pluck your daughter like a flower and bring her to you in this country. Do you understand? Do you have a daughter?"

My mother nodded again and, apparently, listened fascinated to hear this torrent of information, yet was still not sure whether to believe it.

Before the war when we wrote to my mother, auntie Marga always used to address the envelope. Therefore, I never knew or was interested in the address in England to which my aunt sent our letters. However, around the time of my mother's visit to the spiritualist meeting, I suppose, some time in November 1945, suddenly an address came into my mind. As soon as the war had ended, I had wanted to communicate with my mother, but as I never knew her address, I could not write to her.

My knowledge of English at that time was, of course, non-existent and I found it hard to believe that the correct address had come into my mind, but I was clutching at straws. I felt that it was worth taking the risk, sat down immediately and wrote a very long letter, addressing it to 130 Willersley Avenue, Sidcup, Kent, England. In this letter I explained what had happened to us, including my father's death and told her how happy I was with aunt Marga No 2, how I loved the Partisan Gymnasium, where I had so many friends and that I hoped to study philosophy and literature at University after completing my secondary education. I was particularly happy that day for two reasons: firstly, I hoped soon to hear from mama and, perhaps, visit her for a holiday in England and, secondly, because my language teacher, having read the manuscript of my poetry, in Serbo-Croat, of course, said that the poems were good and it might be possible to have them published.

Needless to say, when my mother received my letter, confirming all that the medium had said and more, she nearly had a nervous breakdown. She had to be put to bed and sedated, but gradually she accepted the news after writing to Leslie in Burma and passing all the contents of my letter to him. Ivan, who by now treated my mother almost as his own, was a great solace to her.

Mama immediately decided that she wanted me in England with her and that she and Leslie could offer me their home, so that Ivan and I could be brought up as brother and sister. That we eventually did accept each other as such is in no small way due to Ivan's charm, kindness and love. Not many small boys of twelve would be so magnanimous as to be prepared to accept a sixteen year old ready made sister, with whom it was difficult to communicate, because of the language barrier. A letter was quickly despatched to me to this effect.

After I was over the initial shock, which almost made me refuse the offer of a permanent home in England with my natural mother, I began considering her offer in earnest. All that winter of 1945/46, I had to make the biggest decision of my life: do I join mama who, although idealised in my imagination and poetry was virtually a stranger. I had not lived with her since I was four and had not seen her since I was eight. I can't speak a word of English. On the other hand, I began wondering whether I would, perhaps, be better off with her, wherever she happened to be. I suppose, a tiny flame of the spirit of adventure was becoming lit.

During the next few months Andy was a great help to me, both with the actual business of translating letters from Leslie and Ivan, for he could speak excellent English which he had learnt from his American mother, and also with helping me to weigh up the pros and cons of going to England to live.

The main obstacle to my coming to England to live was the fact that I had set my heart on going to University to study philosophy and literature and could not possibly visualise myself speaking English well enough within a reasonable time, in order to do anything other than a menial job. Little did I know that eventually in my forties I would end up teaching English and other subjects in secondary schools in this country!

My other consideration was auntie Marga No 2 who, having lost her only son so tragically, had offered me her home and love for as long as she lived. However, blood is thicker than water was truer of my decision then than I ever realised. It is true, mama had given me away for the best possible reasons, for my assured future, quelling her maternal feelings, yet I would never have been able to do that with my own children, however much rosier their envisaged future might have been.

After many hours of indecision and doubt, discussions with Andy and many other friends, my love and longing for my mother whom, despite the fact that, through alienation and distance I did not know, but only idealised and idolised, I wrote to tell her that I would like to come as soon as practical and possible. I only wanted to finish the first six months of schooling first. She wrote by return how happy I had made her and that she would do her best, with Leslie's helpful letters from Burma supporting her application to the then Home Secretary, Mr Chuter Ede, for me to enter this country.

I told auntie Marga of my decision and asked her to forgive me for deserting her, thanking her for her love and hospitality. She bravely said she would help me pack and when the time came, did just that. However, she never forgave my mother, wrote her nasty letters and died of a broken heart, so I was told, leaving me an unposted letter, which someone very kindly did not pass on to me. However, while she was still alive we corresponded amicably. Lately, as I have grown older, I have understood even better the heartbreak I must have caused her by leaving. I have often even wondered whether some of my later suffering was sent in just retribution.

When my mother heard that I was willing to come, she started the long and arduous proceedings to get me over here. She visited her local MP, George Wallace, weekly and it was mainly due to his efforts that I was eventually given permission to fly to England in a military Dakota from Belgrade. I still have the written permission signed by Mr Chute Ede.

In these days of private and state airlines, it seems incredible that I had come in an aeroplane with a hole in the middle of the floor, but this was less than a year after the end of World War II.

I finished the first telescoped year at school at the end of

February, said good-bye and good luck to all my colleagues, auntie Jelka, uncle Emil and auntie Marga No 2, and started my journey from Zagreb railway station. No aeroplanes left from Zagreb at that time - I don't even know if it had an airport then - so the first part of my trip to England was by train to Belgrade. There I also had to find the UNRRA offices, in order to be inoculated against something or other and obtain a certificate of proof for it. I cannot remember the meaning of this acronym, except that the first few words were United Nations Rehabilitation etc.

It was with some trepidation that I mounted the train, knowing that I would be completely alone on the journey and, although I would be met on arrival in England, there would be no one I could turn to in Belgrade, where I had to spend three days before getting on the aircraft. As soon as I stepped off the train in this, the largest city in Jugoslavia, I realised I was on my own and just had to get on with it. Luckily, I did not have too much luggage; auntie Marga had had three dresses, a coat and hat made for me and, obviously, I took the manuscript of my poems, as well as some books and a magazine with me. Naturally, also, pictures of my friends and Marshall Tito and my lace confirmation dress.

I hailed a taxi and asked him if he could recommend a suitable hotel for me, after I explained why I was there. One cannot imagine the danger of doing that in this day and age, where corruption, paedophilia, drug culture and other indescribable vices are rife! Then I felt quite safe, as he dropped me in front of a large hotel and waited to see if I managed to book a room for two nights, for that is the time I allowed before catching my 'plane, which mama had booked and paid for in England.

The first night in this strange hotel room was the worst. I had already found UNRRA offices, booked my inoculations for the next day and then walked around the strange city which, after 'White' Zagreb[*], for that is the adjective usually given to the city where I was

---

[*] *called that because at 4 am every morning large lorries tour the city, thoroughly washing all the street.s*

born, seemed to deserve the adjective 'Grey'. Although it was the capital of my country, I had never been there before.

That night, sitting in my room, staring at the dark red walls surrounding me, the enormity of my decision hit me. How could I leave auntie Marga, who had done so much for me and who I knew to be devastated by my departure, although she tried not to show it! What will happen if I don't get on with my mother? Will I like my new country? Will I be able to learn its language, find a suitable school after a while, make new friends, and go to University?

What will happen if Leslie, Ivan and I don't get on or don't like each other? Will I miss my friends and my country too much? Even fifty-eight years after that day I can still smell the newly painted walls in that room and be transported to that time and place!

Most of the rest of my days in Belgrade were spent in cinemas, as far as I can remember, in order that I would not feel too lonely in the hotel room. In between times I went into small restaurants and snack bars for something to eat. Of all the films and cartoons I saw then I cannot remember a single one. I probably fell asleep from exhaustion in many of them, as my nights in the hotel room were spent in contemplation rather than sleep.

Eventually, in possession of all my permits and certificates, I stepped on to the aeroplane and the first leg of my proper journey and big adventure began.

The 'plane was not full and most of the passengers were military personnel. We all sat on wooden seats surrounding that hole in the middle. I was very conscious of it and a little worried that someone would fall through. Whether it was apprehension or motion that made me a little sick I don't know, but my co-passengers were very solicitous and I recovered quite quickly. Although I have travelled reasonably often by aeroplane since, I never feel very safe and would rather travel by other means. I'm fully conscious of the fact that car journeys these days on our overcrowded roads may be more dangerous, but I still prefer to be on terra firma.

After a few hours in flight, apart from a refuelling stop in Bari, we arrived in Naples. The aeroplane developed a fault and we were stuck in Naples for a couple of days. At any other time, I dare say, I would have been overjoyed to be in Naples but, having no money and being anxious to reach England, I did not seem to take in any of its beauty, just the poor state of the buildings we saw. No doubt, the modern city of Naples is vastly different from the poor post war variety.

One memory of Naples etched itself on my mind. At the airport, due to the extreme cold of late February/early March, open fires were lit and that was the first time I had ever seen an open fire. In Croatia, although many places nowadays are centrally heated, at that time, as I suppose for several decades or even centuries, nearly every room in a house or flat was heated by a tall, square structure, called a 'kamin', finished with glazed tiles, usually brown or bronze in colour, which stood in a corner and, more often than not, reached up to the ceiling. Of course, I imagined that my mother's house in Sidcup would be heated in the same way. When I expressed astonishment at the appearance of open fires, the other people on my flight stated that they were sure my mother's house would contain open fires, too. I remonstrated: "My mother doesn't live like a gypsy. She wouldn't dream of having open fires. I'm sure you are mistaken." But they were not, of course!

Mama's and Leslie's house, a typical 1930 semi-detached in Sidcup, had an open fire in each room which, in retrospect, now seems quite normal to me. However, she, too, never could get used to open fires for, although they are welcoming, they scorch your front or your backside, but never keep all of you warm at the same time. She also hated the constant shovelling of coal necessary to keep the open fires burning in those days that, she said, were redolent of living on a ship, constantly having to stoke the boiler. She was very glad when much later they moved to a new, beautiful, detached, centrally heated home in Chislehurst, where the only fire was in the lounge and that was a pretend open fire, heated by gas.

We left Naples for France after the 'plane was repaired and again were stranded in Bordeaux during the fancy dress festivities at the end of February/beginning of March. At least there we saw figures in fancy dress with elaborate masks dancing in the streets of the town.

Meanwhile, Leslie arrived in England during the first week of March from the humid heat of Burma to the icy cold of post war England, in order to be demobbed.

CHAPTER 5
England, Here I Am!

On my sixteenth birthday, 6 March 1946, I landed at Odiham Military Airport in Hampshire and, full of apprehension, trepidation , hope and expectations, I boarded the waiting coach which took me to London and a new life.

Waiting at the coach station, I can still see my mother, who was only 5ft tall, whereas I had expected her to be at least 5ft 8ins! When children are small, their parents always seem gigantically tall. Next to her stood Leslie in his bush hat, the like of which I had never seen.

My mother had a tremendous shock when she saw me. I was dressed in my new brown coat, with a matching brown hat with tassels hanging down, the ones aunt Marga had had made for me, which was the height of fashion in Zagreb circa 1946. As I stepped off the coach into my mother's arms, she fingered the tassels and, believing them to be my brown hair, started crying: "My poor darling! Your hair! Your hair!" This was spoken all in Serbo-Croat, of course, interspersed with fast asides in English to Leslie.

It is funny how foreign languages always sound as if they are spoken much faster than in reality. Certainly, English sounded much faster to me than anything I had ever heard. Mama also could not understand the other well-known fact as practised on her when she first came to England: if a foreigner does not understand something, you shout louder!

Aged 14/15. My confirmation in Zagreb

Early days in England, aged 16,
playing the organ in a church in Welling, Kent

The three of us started to make our way towards Charing Cross Station, in order to catch a Loop line train to Dartford, stopping at Sidcup, when I told mama that I needed to go to the toilet. On being told that there were no nearby toilets and I would have to wait until we reached the Station, I remonstrated: "But, mama, look at all the toilets around here. Can't I go in one of those?", pointing to all the 'Closed' signs in every shop we passed. I thought the word for toilet would be similar to Croatian, which was borrowed from the German: 'Klosett'! When the true English meaning of 'Closed' hanging in the door of every shop was explained to me, I saw the funny side and the ice between the three of us was broken.

My stay in England began well. When we arrived at 130 Willersley Avenue, my first impression of the town was amazement that all the houses in the same road were identical. In the former Jugoslavia, every house was always different, though most people do not live in houses, but rent flats in large blocks.

Waiting at the house, but fast asleep, was my new stepbrother, Ivan, whom I came to know the next morning. That night, as we were all so tired, not a little due to our excitement, after a meal we went to bed.

For my first night, I slept on a divan bed in the dining room and was still fast asleep when I felt someone looking at me. It was Ivan. He had wanted to be present when I woke up, as he had saved many comics for weeks, in order to help me learn English! I certainly received my first few lessons from him using the comics and it was Ivan's enthusiasm and solicitude, which helped me get over any misgivings or loneliness I might have felt.

My mother, of course, wanted to take me everywhere around Sidcup in the next few days. She wanted to tell her neighbours and friends all about her long lost daughter. I remember going shopping with her every day nearby to the Oval neighbourhood shopping centre, when she would introduce me, tell every person she met our whole story, then turn to me and translate what she had related. Gradually, after a few days of hearing my story repeated in English innumerable times, I picked up the relevant words and could say to mama: "You don't need to translate everything to me any more; I've understood."

It never ceases to amaze me that my mother and I became so close so quickly and that Leslie and Ivan also accepted me as a daughter and sister so readily. Of course I, in turn, was very happy and grateful to be a member of a real family unit, after all that had happened to me. Ivan was at school all day, whilst I spent my time going shopping with mama, going to the swimming pool at nearby Eltham and sitting at home knitting simple lace tablecloths or trying to make sense of English newspapers. The Daily Mirror, actually, to which Leslie subscribed, as he liked Cassandra, the famous column writer.

The reason I had to knit tablecloths, apart from the fact that mama liked the look of the finished articles and because she did not knit or crochet, was because I had no knitting patterns in my own language and, as yet, could not understand English ones.

After about six weeks in England, my English was nearly fluent enough for us to consider making arrangements for me to start school in September.

As I had passed my 11+ in the former Jugoslavia and had attended a Grammar type school, one of our neighbours suggested that we contact the Headmistress of the local Grammar School, Chislehurst and Sidcup County Grammar School for Girls, with a view to my joining it at the beginning of the next academic year.

THE PHOTOGRAPH

I am 16 today!
Just arrived in England
frightened, apprehensive
eager to be happy.
The 'plane which brought me here
an old military Dakota -
a hole in the middle of the floor,
daunting and dangerous.
As I stepped off
my mother and her husband
were waiting.

"My poor darling, your hair!",
the first words she spoke to me!
It was not my hair,
It was the raggedy tassel
on my new pillbox hat
that confused her;
my hair underneath
was normal, like me.

My mother's new husband,
demobbed from Burma
the day before,
wore a funny bush hat
when he took our photograph.

Doesn't mama look tiny, I thought;
I hadn't seen her since I was eight -
she was tall then.

I am eager to learn the language
of my new country!
I hope this land will accept me
as happily as I accept
its challenge
and its welcome.

We made an appointment for the next day. I was a little nervous, though very eager and only later realised how very lucky I was to meet Miss Huxstep, our wonderful and visionary Headmistress at that time, to whom I have never ceased to be grateful. I really don't know how I would have fared if she had not greeted me so warmly.

After establishing that my English was, according to me, 'fluent', and asking me several pertinent questions regarding my knowledge of mathematics and other subjects, Miss Huxstep invited me to come to school "tomorrow". As I didn't know the names of any mathematical operations, I remember writing down two simultaneous equations to show my latest knowledge of that subject.

I panicked. September was the month I intended starting and it was only some time at the end of April or beginning of May. There was so much English I could and ought to learn in the meantime, in order to make me better prepared to cope with the challenges I knew I would have to confront. However, Miss Huxstep, from her wide experience of learning and wise counsel, was adamant. "Tomorrow is as good as next September, my dear, and it is much nearer." So tomorrow it was.

Once more I was so lucky with my new set of friends with many of whom now, nearly sixty years later, I still correspond and see, even those who have been living abroad for many years. One such friend, Dell (Audrey), comes to England for a few weeks occasionally from Canada and we meet in London for a day when we can. Even after many years we feel immediately as if we had been meeting frequently throughout the years. One year we met in Covent Garden and giggled companionably when I introduced her to the indecent luxury of a sundae at the Rock Garden Cafe. The sundaes there are so sumptuous they are indescribable; in fact, while we were eating our joint mega sundae, some Norwegian tourists insisted on taking our photograph.

Another school friend, Gwen, now lives in New Zealand, but we still write to each other and she came over to this country twice in the last five years and on the first occasion stayed with us.

There are numerous other school friends, who live in this country, with whom I am often still in touch, such as Sheila Willmoth and Gwyneth Dempster. Sheila and her husband, Peter, as well as their whole family are dear to us.

My life and experiences had made me grow up long before my time, but when I became a pupil at Chislehurst, I gradually recovered my lost childhood. Leslie succinctly put it once when I was being silly for a change: "When you arrived in this country, you were a very grown up young lady, but now you are just a silly, giggling English schoolgirl, like all the others!" That is probably why I survived unscathed.

The only visual reminder of my past at that time was a photograph of President Tito, which I insisted should occupy pride of place in my bedroom. Needless to say, it was discarded as soon as I acquired a photograph of any current boyfriend.

The girls at school were divided into three camps: all were very friendly and helpful, but some behaved as if I could never be accepted on an equal footing, as I was just a foreigner, whilst others were crazy about anyone foreign and monopolised me. The vast majority accepted and treated me as one of them, teaching me the correct pronunciation of some words which I had learnt from mama, whose pronunciation, as mentioned before was, at times, questionable.

One of these words I particularly remember was 'now', which mama and later I pronounced as 'nehw'. My best friends, Audrey and June, would say to me: "Say, 'now'", to which I would reply

"Nehw".

They would then say: "Say 'cow'."

"Cow"

"Say 'brow'."

"Brow."

"Say 'now'."

"Nehw."

Then we would all dissolve into laughter. Eventually, I realised what they wanted me to say and that mama did not speak the perfect English I thought she did, but it was still better than mine at the time! She was just a little too old when she came to this country to lose the accent she acquired.

For many years afterwards there were very occasional words which I mispronounced and the two which stick in my mind are: epitome and jeopardise. I used to pronounce them 'epitom' and 'joppardise', until I learnt better.

The teachers also were very good and kind, particularly my form teacher Miss Higgins, who taught history and had to slow down her dictation, at times almost to a standstill, in order that I could cope and cope I did.

For many years I also heard from Miss Milton, my German teacher and the form mistress of my sixth form. She has sadly now died, but lived into her nineties. Miss Huxstep, too, corresponded with me through the years and died in a nursing home in her nineties. Right up to the end I heard from her and sent her Christmas gifts. She loved to hear all about my family and liked to be brought up to date with news of her 'old girls'.

There are many memories of those first days and months at my wonderful Grammar School, such as picnics with my class in Blackheath Park, Sunday teas at my friend June's house, where I tried to call her cat 'Tigger' instead of Tiger. Also, I remember the time I picked a dandelion and June and Audrey laughed, but were too shy and embarrassed to tell me that "it is said that if you pick this weed you'll wet the bed."When I did eventually drag it out of them, I remember saying: "Is that all? That's nothing!"

Another memory of that time was being told off by Miss Carr, the Domestic Science teacher, for keeping my left hand touching the table and not on my lap while I was eating. In Europe, it is impolite to keep your hand on your lap, but one must keep it on the table in such a fashion that the wrist is touching the edge of the table, the hand gently touching the surface; therefore, I felt very aggrieved, nay, indignant, at being told off for something I thought was correct.

School lunches were very monotonous; usually they consisted of some kind of stew, followed by chocolate pudding and thick custard. I didn't know what to do with the tiny bones, which each mouthful of stew provided; I was afraid to put them out of my mouth onto the plate, so I used to wrap them in the corner of my handkerchief unobtrusively, pretending I was blowing my nose. My mother told me later that she was very worried when she found those in the hankie!

No one knew into which form I should be placed. My English vocabulary at the beginning was no richer than a playgroup child's, yet my knowledge and intelligence were commensurate with my age apparently, in most subjects except Geography. According to those who know me, that is my Achilles' heel. I dispute this at my present age, but I expect it was true then.

When it was decided to place me in the top A form of the Lower Fifth class and enter me for the Lower Fifth Summer examinations, about a fortnight or a month after I joined the school, just to see what I could do, I was excited, overjoyed, apprehensive and panic-stricken, all at the same time. I had never had a proper examination, except for the 11+.

Apart from 'Little Matriculation' and 'Big Matriculation', which were taken after four and eight years of secondary schooling respectively, there were no other examinations taken by pupils in Jugoslavia at that time. Assessment was by constant random oral questioning in class in each subject, homework marks and frequent oral testing on topics. One had to learn everything thoroughly for each lesson, in case one was asked a question and the mark noted. I am not sure which is the better system, examinations and tests, as well as homework and oral questioning in class, but with no marks noted for questions asked, or the old Jugoslav system, with no written examinations, but being judged throughout the year on verbal answers in class on all topics and all written work handed in.

One had to learn thoroughly each topic, in order to gain a good mark when questioned in class. The marks accorded, including on reports, were as follows:

5	excellent
4	very good
3	good
2	satisfactory
1	unsatisfactory

All the marks counted and were averaged for the yearly report, which was issued at the end of the scholastic year in June.

The school year usually started on 1 September and ended on the last day in June, thus giving everyone a long summer holiday. There were no terms or half terms, just short breaks for Christmas and Easter, with occasional days off for Saints' days and public holidays.

I can honestly say I had never had a mark of less than 5, for both attainment and effort, except for PE, for which I usually had 5 for effort and 3 for attainment! I never could run fast and most of PE in those days in Jugoslavia consisted of running. It was only when I came to an English school and later when I left school and joined the Bank that I played a lot of sport, particularly tennis, netball, hockey and did a lot of swimming. However, nowadays, my main sport, or should I say hobby, is caravanning with my husband and family. as well as yoga, line-dancing and aqua-aerobics.

Well, to cut a long story short, I was entered for all the Lower Fifth internal examinations: English, Maths, History, German, English Literature, Biology, Physics with Chemistry, Geography, barely a month after joining the school and less than three months after arriving in England! Although, of course, my marks could not be compared with someone who was born in England and attended the school for any length of time, everyone appeared pleased with me, despite my very low marks. That is, everyone, except the Geography teacher, Miss Knight.

In the Geography examination, for one of the questions we were given a photograph and a map and we had to say where we thought the photograph was taken. I was very pleased with myself, as I was convinced I knew exactly the spot where the photographer stood, a place called 'Inn'. I handed in my paper with a smug expression and, when I told my friends of my success, they laughed. Apparently, the map was covered with places called 'Inn'! All the pubs in the neighbourhood were there. I could see the joke, when I realised what I had done, but I was wisely advised to drop Geography 'O' level. Hence, from then on my total knowledge of the subject has been almost limited to the geography of Jugoslavia, counties of England and capitals of the world! Nowadays, of course, enriched by the names of all the places in Europe, Canada and America which I have visited.

After the examinations, I continued in the Lower Fifth A form until the end of term, which was the end of the school year and then went up into the Upper Fifth year with them, leaving me nine months until my School Certificate.

I threw myself wholeheartedly into the life of the school, joining many societies, such as the Philistines, Debating, History and others and restarted learning the piano. It was, in fact, one of my greatest joys to find that we had a piano at home in Sidcup, which had belonged to Leslie's parents, and that after so many years without one I could again have lessons. I remember getting half a crown (2s 6d), per week pocket money, most of which was spent on sheet music, mainly current pop and classical music books. I still have some of them, though the tunes, such as Slow Boat to China, Beautiful Dreamer, etc, would not exactly be my choice now. Some, on the other hand, have become popular for the second or even the third time.

The next year passed very quickly and in June 1947, I took my 'O' levels or, rather, my School Certificate as it was known then, obtaining several Distinctions and Credits, thus qualifying for Matriculation exemption. The following year I added three more 'B' grades, including separate Physics and Chemistry, as I had only taken the joint subject Physics with Chemistry originally.

Everyone, including me, was overjoyed with my success and on Speech Day Miss Huxstep kindly told all those present how proud the school was of my unusual achievement, much to my mother 's pride and joy. I cannot help but feel that it was purely a testament to the School's excellent teaching and my friends' untiring help and devotion, that enabled me to succeed and gain the Matriculation Certificate, after such a brief term of schooling and learning English.

I particularly enjoyed English Literature and, despite the fact that I had been in England only fifteen months when I took the examination, I obtained a 'B' grade in this due, in no small measure to Miss White, our English teacher . We were lucky, I feel, to study 'Macbeth', the First World War poets and Jane Austin's 'Pride and Prejudice', all of which have remained my favourite pieces of English literature since then.

The very first English poem I learnt by heart was Rupert Brooke's 'Soldier'. It seems curious to me now that even before I became naturalised English and 100 per cent attached to this country, I was able to recite, with feeling, the opening lines of that famous poem:

"If I should die, think only this of me,
That there's some corner of a foreign field
That is forever England."

I also learnt by heart large chunks of Macbeth and ever since have never tired of seeing it performed, whether as a school play or at Stratford-upon-Avon, with someone like Dame Judi Dench as Lady Macbeth.

As foreign languages at "O' level, I sat German and Serbo-Croat. The latter was a very interesting and enjoyable experience, fraught with excitement and fear. Supposing I do badly in this one subject in which I should excel?

As the only candidate sitting the Serbo-Croat examination, I was installed in the smaller of the two staff rooms at the school, which contained just the invigilator and me. The hay fever season was in full swing, as usual at examination time and I was, therefore, in full flood: sneezing, nose running, eyes streaming. The prose translation from Serbo-Croat was a doddle and the poem to be translated was beautiful. I also enjoyed writing the simple essay that was required and which could, of course, cause some difficulty to someone who had to learn the language as a foreigner. The translation from English into Serbo-Croat, however, gave me some difficulty and a few anxious moments. It was obviously an extract from a famous English literary work, only I had never read it: ". . . woke up to find the sun shining, the sky serene." I knew very well how to translate "woke up to find the sun shining", but, God in heaven, what does "the sky serene" mean? Is it a special name given to a particular cloud formation in the sky? I spent a long time on this phrase and luckily collected myself in time to finish translating the rest of the extract, which was quite lengthy, and was eventually rewarded with an A grade in both Serbo-Croat and German. Eventually I found out that my mark for Serbo-Croat was 98 per cent, as I wrote to the examiner much later, to ask for details of the original poem in the paper.

A few months later I was choosing a book in the local library in Sidcup, when I felt particularly drawn to a bookshelf round a corner, the works of Aldous Huxley. The first book I drew out was entitled Chrome Yellow. It fell open on the first page of a chapter somewhere in the middle of the book and, to my amazement, I read: ". . . woke up to find the sun shining, the sky serene." What a coincidence! For so long I had wondered from where the extract had been taken, especially now that I had learnt the meaning of the phrase and was rewarded with the answer.

It was a great pity that, although my English was excellent for the length of time I had been learning it, it was not good enough for me to study it at 'A' level, together with other languages or arts subjects and, therefore, I decided that I wanted to be a research chemist and studied Chemistry, Physics, Biology and Pure Mathematics in the Sixth Form.

We all revelled being grown up enough, in our opinion, to be members of the Sixth Form, especially as one of my best friends, June, became Head Girl. We travelled to other schools for debates, visited the Science Museum for courses, went to dances to which the boys from the Boys' Grammar School were invited.

The Electron exhibition at the Science Museum particularly drew me to the museum every day for a week and I began to love sciences after all.

At one of the dances held jointly with the Boys' school, I met a boy called Jim from Orpington, who almost immediately left for

Melbourne, Australia, with his family. We corresponded for a while, then stopped. He was my first English boyfriend.

During the Lower Sixth year, my mother wanted to become a naturalised British subject and was keen, of course, for me to be naturalised at the same time. I also wanted this, but remember hating to wear my school uniform, especially school beret, to the office in London. Mama thought it would make a good impression when they discovered that I was an English schoolgirl!

In the summer of that year, just like the year after, my friend Audrey's parents, Mr and Mrs Marchant, asked me to spend a few weeks with them and Audrey at their beach hut in Seasalter in Kent. I was so happy, as we could swim every day in the sea, where waves were high and exciting. In the evenings we used to go to play snooker or pool and have a drink, though I'm sure it was nothing stronger than lemonade. We also used to play rounders with two boys from Rickmansworth called Gordon and Chas, who seemed much older, though I'm sure were only a year or two older than we were. One very exciting day Audrey and I were allowed to go to another seaside resort with a boy on his motorcycle and sidecar, taking it in turns to pillion ride. It felt very daring!

Time seemed to go by very fast. When I was in the Upper Sixth, I applied to several Universities and University Colleges, of which my main and favourite was Leicester. I was pleased to be offered an interview and was thrilled that, following my attendance, they offered me a place whether I passed my 'A' levels or not. At that time, one could retake these at the College, if members of the Board interviewing the student believed the student had exceptional potential.

Leicester itself made a very good impression on me. The main street with its clocktower had certain charm and the shops seemed exciting. The University College that was, which is now Leicester University, despite the fact that it was located opposite a cemetery, looked welcoming and so did the members of the interviewing Board, who were very thorough in their questioning. I told them that I wanted to do research chemistry, perhaps dealing with food or drugs/medicines, but that I was willing to be advised on the best course to take. When they told me of their decision, after making me wait outside for a little while, I thanked them and started the long journey back.

Although I was thrilled to be accepted, after a while I still hankered after Arts subjects and found the Sciences not as easy as I had at first thought. I know that my brain does not work on logical/mathematical lines and is happier working out a rhyme or metaphor, than reasoning out problems. In addition, mama and Leslie had impressed on me that if and when I attended University, I would have to study hard and would not have time for boyfriends, theatre trips and other luxuries. Therefore, it was not surprising that about a week before the 'A' level results were due, I wrote to the then Big Five Banks, asking whether they had any clerical vacancies. All five replied favourably, offering me interviews, but as Barclays Bank's was first, I attended this.

I remember the Personnel Manager telling me that if I stayed a minimum of five years, I would be given a dowry, according to the number of years served. At that time, five years seemed an eternity and, although I smiled gratefully at the information on the bounty offered, I thought privately to myself: "I wonder where I'll be at the end of five years? Probably married, with a couple of children!" In actual fact I stayed seven years and was very grateful for the £200 odd dowry I did eventually receive.

The Personnel Manager offered me a job as a clerk in the Securities Department (Coupon Section) of their Chief Foreign Branch, at 168 Fenchurch Street, EC3, starting on 19 September 1949. I then wrote to the other four banks, advising them that I had accepted the job at Barclays. I was very surprised and pleased to receive a letter wishing me good luck in my new job, both from the old Westminster Bank and Lloyds. I cannot imagine that happening today when even applications for jobs often do not receive acknowledgements!

I started my job in Barclays on the appointed day, which seemed to me to be the least propitious day for starting work in a bank: the day the £ was devalued! Despite that inauspicious beginning, I was very happy at work there, especially as I was lucky enough to move through other departments in the Foreign Branch and, therefore, never became bored with the daily routine. Had I stayed long in the coupon section, however, I'm sure I would have become very bored in time. The first friend I made in my new job was a girl called Genia Brougham, who was a little unusual and told me that one of her ancestors had invented a form of transport called a brougham, which I believe is somewhat like the French fiacre, the conveyance we had used to take us to the vineyard in Slavonski Brod. She appeared to be someone whose family had known better fortune and had fallen on hard times.

My stay in the Securities Department was pretty uneventful, except for one evening in January 1950. It was the custom in the Department for all the coupon sheets which had not been dealt with, ie their worth not calculated, to be collected and placed at about 4.45 pm into a very large metal trunk. This was then taken by lift, accompanied by the messenger, into the safe. That night I had done this with my unfinished coupons, as usual, and then left to catch a train home to Sidcup from Cannon Street Station. I entered my usual compartment and, as I always knitted on the train, I unzipped my knitting bag and . . . . . instead of two knitting needles, half a jumper front and a ball of wool, I was faced with a roll of uncut coupons, worth thousands of pounds, encashable on demand! I had obviously carefully packed my knitting into the appropriate envelope, which was placed in the strongbox and accompanied by the messenger to the safe in the vaults!

I froze, frightened even to breathe, but had the presence of mind to close the zip quickly noticed by no one. I then sat quietly, still in a state of shock, until the train pulled into Sidcup. Had my mistake been discovered, who would have believed my innocence and attributed the presence of the coupons to my absent-mindedness and carelessness, not to premeditated, planned stealing?

When I came off the train, I was extremely careful crossing the road to the bus stop; I did not dare risk getting run over. As soon as I arrived home, I told my mother and we stuck a piece of paper stating: "Don't forget!", in Croatian on my dressing table, just in case I forgot my bag in the morning.

After an uneventful journey to work the next morning, thank goodness, I managed to get my knitting out of the safe, still in its coupon envelope, quite unobserved and with my heart beating fast. I could not relate this story to anyone for years, but did confess it, amid laughter, on the day I left the bank to get married.

As soon as I joined the bank, I enrolled in evening classes at the local Technical School, in order to learn typewriting and shorthand. I was particularly keen to learn typewriting as quickly as possible, in order to be more versatile and able to move around to other Departments. Therefore, I attended two evenings per week for typing and one for shorthand. At Christmas, after just over two months, I passed RSA Typewriting Examination Stage I, at Easter Stage II and followed this with Stage III and 100 wpm shorthand.

Aged 21 - Photograph taken at the Bank

My next department in the bank was Outward Credits, where I made so many friends, almost too numerous to mention. Whilst there, I attended the weddings of the best of these, John Budd and also Ann and Tony Falvey. I still correspond with a lot of the 'girls' from the Bank, some now retired. My male colleagues there have risen high up the ladder, Tony reaching the position of Joint General Manager of Chief Foreign Branch, from which position he has now retired.

Around 1953 I was thrilled to receive a letter from my schoolfriend, Andy, from Aberystwyth, telling me that he was spending a year there at the end of his medical studies and that he could spend a week in London. I was overjoyed and insisted that he stayed with us in Sidcup. I really looked forward to seeing my old friend after so many years and showing him around London, but was quite unprepared for the love which I still felt for him and which he seemed to reciprocate on our meeting. It was wonderful to see him again, stroll through St James' Park hand in hand and converse in English this time. However, Andy had grown up a lot and whereas he would, perhaps, have been quite prepared for a brief interlude, I was not. Therefore, we have remained very good friends and when we married other people a year or two later, our friendship became even stronger. I like his wife very much and I think he likes my husband equally.

As mentioned before, the times were different when I was young and even at 22 years of age, I had to ask even beg permission from mama and Leslie to stay away from home, especially where a boy might have been concerned. To illustrate this, I remember the particular weekend of Frank's Old Boys' Reunion Dance. Frank was an officer in the Kenya Police, who was on leave in the United Kingdom for six months and whom I met at a dance in Eltham at the beginning of his leave. We had been going out most evenings and at weekends for several months, when his old school at Egham in Surrey had a reunion dance. This was to be held on a Friday evening until 1 am and, as Frank did not have a car in this country, he suggested that he would book two rooms for us in the adjoining hotel, the Pack Horse.

Knowing everything would be 'above board' in the parlance of the time, I did not expect quite the furore and objections that this suggestion provoked. For days after I asked if I could go, both mama and Leslie gave an emphatic "No". I cried, remonstrated, schemed, begged. Eventually, knowing that I was in the right, I worked out exactly what I was going to say to my mother: "Mama, most girls of my age would not ask permission, but would just go. I would rather you gave me permission, but if you don't, I've decided I'm old enough to go and will go, even if you don't agree."

Faced with this reasonable ultimatum at my age, mother and Leslie consented. Frank and I had a wonderful time and the dinner that night was delicious. My bedroom was luxurious but, when I fell into bed tired after a day's work in the bank, followed by an evening's dancing, I naturally pressed the bedside light switch. No light came on. However, the next minute there was a knock at the door with a gentlemen offering me room service, much to my embarrassment. I had obviously pressed the wrong switch and had summoned unwanted help instead of light in my darkness.

In the morning I had the biggest surprise of the lot. Whereas the dining room the night before was cosy with thick velvet curtains closed, in the morning the curtains were pulled back to reveal a glass wall, or patio doors, as they would be known now. Through the glass one could see a beautiful, breathtaking view of the river Thames, which seemed barely a yard or two away. I have never enjoyed breakfast as much before or since and was so glad I came. During the past twenty years or so I have often tried to find this dining room again, but only managed to find a different Pack Horse in Egham and this certainly was not situated on the banks of the Thames. Perhaps it was all a dream?

I used to spend many Saturday afternoons and evenings in

London, attending classical concerts and plays in theatres, often in the cheapest seats at two shillings and sixpence, in the gallery, the equivalent of approximately 13p; sometimes even standing in the 'standing room only' places a the back of the stalls. On these occasions I would go with friends or on my own. When I went on my own, I often met exceptionally interesting and charming people, usually girls of my own age from abroad, who were either studying here or, having finished their University education in their own country, on a trip given to them by their parents as a reward for their degree. I loved showing them round London and would often take them to my parents' home for a meal. They appreciated being part of a family again, if only briefly, after being alone perhaps in the Metropolis. One such girl was from South Africa and we corresponded for many years after she returned home.

My friends and I often queued for the Proms and I still feel the excitement and the patriotism swell up as they did each year that I was lucky enough to go to the last night of the Proms! I also attended several concerts when Eileen Joyce was the soloist; Cyril Smith and his wife, Phyllis Selick were my favourites, too. I greatly admired Cyril Smith's courage when he played the concerto for one hand after his stroke. Never did I dream then that I would also have a stroke one day, long before I was 50.

As soon as I could type well, I was moved to Exchange Control Department, where the Emigration Section proved quite interesting. I became departmental secretary and, having learnt shorthand and typewriting, joined two new evening classes: French and Philosophy. It strikes me as funny now that, every time I had a boyfriend at that time and we broke up, I decided to join an evening class and learn something new. I can almost count the number of boyfriends I had by the number of subjects I learnt at evening classes, in addition to shorthand and typewriting: French, Russian, Philosophy, Modern Science.

The most enjoyable classes were French and Russian at

Goldsmith's College, New Cross, because after these, nearly the whole class, plus lecturers, adjourned to the 'Rosemary Branch' next door, in order to continue discussion! Indirectly, it was the French class at Goldsmith's that was eventually responsible for my meeting Graham, although the connection is very tenuous.

A boy in our French class, Frank, asked me out to a New Year's Eve party, 31 December 1954. However, once we had arrived at the party, he found another girl, while a boy called Reg asked me out to the theatre the following week. Reg and I subsequently went out for a few months and arranged to go to Brittany on holiday in the summer. However, a short while before we were due to go, he decided that he did not want to go out with me any more and wanted to go on holiday to Dinard by himself. Therefore, I went to the Workers' Travel Association (WTA), the well- known travel agents at that time and asked if I could change to another party holiday. There were two available: Torquay and Jersey. Luckily, I chose Jersey and found myself on the platform at Waterloo Station, on Friday evening, 17 June 1955.

CHAPTER 6
A Partner For Life

The railways had been on strike during the week commencing 13 June 1955 and all the people who had booked a holiday in Jersey at the end of that week had emergency instructions to go by coach. However, the strike was unexpectedly settled and we were assembled at Waterloo Railway Station. I noticed a handsome young man sitting on a bench nearby with a label matching mine: Sarum Hotel, St Helier, Jersey. Unbeknown to me, this certain young man also noticed me and my luggage with identical labels. When the time came for us to get on to the train, the young man and I, together with one other girl, entered the same compartment marked WTA and we all started to talk.

During the conversation I diffidently voiced my fears that I would be seasick all night. The young man, on the other hand, said that the sea journey was the best part of the whole holiday. We did not exchange names even when we discovered that we worked for rival banks, he for the Westminster (which later became Nat/West, after amalgamation with the National Provincial Bank), and I, of course, for Barclays. We discovered afterwards that, until then, we would never go out with people who worked in banks!

When we embarked, the young man asked the other girl, Edna, and me if we would like a coffee. I very much wanted to accept his offer, but felt unable to, as Edna did not want to go and I did not want to seem forward. Therefore, we said "Good night!", and retired.

I carefully took my anti-seasickness pills, lay down on my bunk and was just about to go to sleep, when Edna began to be very seasick. Cocksure that my tablets had worked wonders and I was, therefore, fine, I suggested that I pass her one of my pills. She agreed. However, the minute I moved, I, too, became very seasick, which state continued for most of the night. The sound of the engine imprinted the jingle "That boy said 'this is the best part of the holiday', that boy said 'this is the best part of the holiday', that boy said . . . ", on my brain, all night long.

As we approached Jersey, the sea became calm and I managed to get up, wash and go up on to the deck. There, refreshed after a good night's sleep, was the young man from Waterloo Station, who volunteered his name, Graham, and asked if I had slept as well as he had? We then watched together a most beautiful sunrise and slowly entered the harbour of St Helier.

The coach waiting to transport the intending residents of the Sarum Hotel stood at the quayside expectantly, but we were not meant to catch it. By the time all the others destined for the hotel were on board, my luggage could not be found. In order not to let me stay behind on my own, Graham very gallantly waited with me until my cases turned up, half an hour later. We, therefore, arrived together at the hotel, the only occupants of the massive coach, which delivered us, to be greeted by the proprietors with the words: "Are you Mr and Mrs Peacock?" When they heard that we were not, they remonstrated: "But you did not book together!" We said we had only just met.

After settling in our rooms - Edna and I shared a room, as we had booked singly - we went down to lunch. Edna had already sat down and there were two seats left at another table for three. Therefore, Graham and I sat down and ate our first meal together. We continued to sit at the same table for the duration of the holiday, sharing it with a lady called Margie.

As soon as we had had our lunch, Edna, Graham and I went into town to explore. We walked for miles and had our first photograph taken together. As I always felt that I was too short and wore smart high heels, when we returned I mentioned I had blisters on both my feet. Graham was very solicitous, but even I was quite unprepared for the 'bloody mess' literally that appeared on the back of my heels and on my squashed toes. For the rest of the holiday I could only wear a pair of flat espadrilles for walking, until my feet recovered.

The first week of the holiday flew by. As soon as Edna realised that Graham and I were an item, in fact, after the first afternoon in town, she did her own thing and Graham and I went everywhere on our own. We visited the different bays on the island, smiled when the wife of the proprietor always called me 'Blossom', danced the evenings away at the hotel dances and won the three-legged race on Sports Day on the beach. I don't know exactly when we fell in love, but we were definitely sure on Friday evening. It was then that Graham told me he had only come for a week and had to go back the next day. He said our romance and our love for each other had been so beautiful and so perfect that if we met again after the holiday we might find it was too good to last and have our dream shattered. Therefore, he was reluctant to ask me for my address. On the other hand, I pleaded more ardently than I had ever pleaded before, that we must meet again, that if he was right we had nothing to lose, but if it turned out that our love was of the lasting kind, we had everything to gain. We both then dissolved in tears of happiness, exchanging our addresses and telephone numbers. I often wonder had we been young and in love in these permissive times, whether the outcome would have been the same?

The next morning Graham and I met for an early breakfast. I accompanied him to the harbour on the hotel coach and watched him catch the boat to the mainland. It was very hard to kiss him good-bye, but I knew that he would be waiting for me at Waterloo Station on my return a week later.

**Our first photograph taken together
Jersey, June 1955**

Resting after winning the 3-legged race
Jersey, June 1955

The following week, of course, time dragged. I could hardly wait for next Saturday to come, although my week was enlivened by telephone calls from Graham in Harlow on alternate evenings and beautiful love letters every day. I, too, spent most days writing letters to him.

Exactly at the expected time the following Saturday my train pulled into Waterloo Station and I ran into Graham's arms. It seemed an eternity since we said goodbye the Saturday before. Hand in hand we walked to the nearest cafe for a cup of tea, which we drank as we gazed into each other's eyes. The poem, which is printed at the beginning of this book, seems to have been written with us in mind and it certainly was true for us at that moment.

Just as we were about to sit down, Graham reached into the pocket of his raincoat which he was carrying, pulled out a small box and half a dozen red roses, all squashed and said: "These are for you", handing them both over. Never have I been so thrilled with such gifts. I still have a pressed rose from that bouquet 49 years later.

The little box contained a gold cross and chain, which I always wear and treasure. When we finished our tea, Graham saw me off onto a train for Sidcup. Having completed a fond farewell, I fell into the train seat tired from the long journey, but so happy to know that nothing had changed. Our love had survived our first separation! I looked round the carriage. Laughing in one corner were two of my best friends from school! From then on, every time we were out in London, we seemed to meet at least one friend from my schooldays. As I went to a reasonably small school with around 700 pupils at that time, I suppose, or maybe even a couple of hundred less, Graham, I'm sure, did not believe that all the people we seemed to meet went to my school!!!

I thought I had carefully avoided mentioning anything about Graham in my letters to mama and Leslie. However, as soon as I arrived home, I was determined to tell them all about him. I was, therefore, astonished that they knew I had met someone because, as Leslie put it: "You said: 'We took part in Sports Day on the beach and won the three-legged race' in your letter. We knew you were not running that kind of race by yourself!"

We arranged that Graham would come for lunch to us the next day, Sunday, and we would go for a drive in the country. Was that a whole fifteen hours away, I remember thinking?

Thank goodness, Graham, mama, Leslie and Ivan liked each other instantly.

From that day on, until we married, we spent alternate weekends at each other's houses. Luckily, I believe, Graham's parents liked me as much and I loved coming to Harlow for weekends. Graham, too, enjoyed spending time in Sidcup.

As soon as I returned to the Bank from holiday, I found a message from Reg, my ex-boyfriend, asking me to meet him for lunch at the famous large building in the city where he worked. Out of curiosity I went and was confronted with a sob story. He had had a dreadful holiday; it was all a mistake and could we, please, get back together, as he really and truly loved me. No chance! I told him what a wonderful boy I had met and what a fabulous holiday we had had, even visiting Dinard for a day by aeroplane from Jersey, where he was. I did not mention the lunch we had there, which included a fat worm on the lettuce. I told him that I had probably met my lasting love, whom I would eventually marry. His parting shot was: "I'll probably send you a bomb for your wedding present." Luckily, in the event, he did not send us anything.

Graham was at Spitalfields Branch at that time and I worked only a short distance away in the city. We telephoned each other at home every day and wrote daily letters, sometimes having them delivered by Bank Messengers, if our branches were on their delivery route.

Apart from weekends at each other's houses and occasional brief lunchtime meetings, we met one evening during each week after work and spent these evenings walking around London, then having a light snack in the Black and White Snack Bar opposite Liverpool Street Station. Occasionally we would go to the theatre, but I always had to see Graham off, instead of vice versa, because his train left at around 10.45 pm, whereas mine left at around midnight. I would then walk to London Bridge Station, get on the train and write him a letter. When I eventually arrived home, I would ring him to say I had arrived back safely. London must have been a much safer place then, for I would never dare walk by myself around Liverpool Street Station or London Bridge at night nowadays.

Both Graham and I had a few days' holiday left and we decided we would go away to Bournemouth on 15 October. We really looked forward to the break and booked two rooms in a boarding house. When we arrived, we were quite pleased with the accommodation.

The landlady was very friendly, but we had to laugh at the elaborate chaperoning technique she employed. Every night when we went to bed, she would follow us at a discrete distance while we kissed goodnight on the landing. Then we would separate and she would shout 'Goodnight' to us. We would each go to our separate little rooms and dream about each other.

On the first night in Bournemouith, we had decided we would go to the 'Grand Ball' at the Winter Gardens. I had brought with me my long yellow halterneck lace evening dress which, with the matching bolero, had been my bridesmaid's dress at two weddings: that of my friend Pepita's from the bank, and my best friend's Pamela's wedding. We walked in feeling grand and then looked round. I was the only lady dressed in evening dress. The others were dressed more suitably for a village hop. It was too late to go back to change, so we pretended that we were correct and they were all wrong. After a valiant effort at pretending to be enjoying ourselves we left, climbed into Graham's car and drove to the seafront to look out over the sea. The weather was freezing; it must have been the coldest October on record. Graham was very quiet. Suddenly, he said: "If only we were on a ship, I would ask the captain to marry us. It would save buying hot water bottles, wouldn't it?" He continued: "Will you marry me, please, darling?" As in all reputable fairy tale love stories, I melted into his arms, whispering: "I will! Do you mean it?" "Of course, I do! I would not joke about something so important!"

The fiasco of an evening turned out wonderful after all!

After gazing at the starlit sky and the moonlit sea through the windscreen for a little while longer, we drove back to the boarding house. The proprietor, who must have been lonely in the late autumn and winter months, was waiting for us. "Would you like to come and have a drink with me?" We gratefully accepted his kind invitation for us to celebrate our engagement.

The next day we went to an ice-cold cinema, where we were the only patrons to freeze through a performance long since forgotten. We also bought the first item for our 'bottom drawer', a 7-piece fruit set. It was cream with blue polka dots, now long broken and not remembered as very tasteful, but a cheap bargain in the sale, which was all we could afford at the time.

Just as we left the shop, Graham asked: "By the way, how old are you, darling?"

"Twenty-five, I replied. "How old are you?"

"Twenty-two, nearly twenty-three", said Graham.

"I thought so", I answered.

Neither of us really worried about each other's ages, when there were so many more important facts to learn and get used to. We had then known each other four months, but were never more sure that we wanted to spend the rest of our lives together.

When my friend, Pamela, became engaged, I remember thinking: poor girl, she will never be able to kiss another man as long as she lives! When Graham and I became engaged, the thought which ran through my mind was: What a lucky girl I am! I'll never have to kiss another man as long as I live!

The following day we left Bournemouth for home and arrived in Sidcup for Graham to ask mama's permission to marry me. Leslie was abroad on business at the time. I remember mama chatting, as always, nineteen to the dozen and not letting Graham get a word in edgeways, while he patiently tried to ask her for my hand in marriage. Eventually, when she stopped speaking for a second, he blurted it out. She was overjoyed, kissed him and me and talked even more, mainly to say how happy she was. Although I know she loved me very much, even to her dying day I think she loved Graham more. For this I was profoundly grateful. Not only had I found a good husband, but mama and Leslie had found another son.

Graham's parents were also very pleased with our engagement and offered to buy us a present or give us a beautiful fine bone china coffee set, which Graham had always coveted. Of course, we chose the latter.

The Harlow of those days - 1955 - was completely different from the Harlow of today. One could walk along muddy paths from Edinburgh Way to First Avenue, where there were no houses beyond the Stow, which served as the main shopping centre of the town. The Town Centre was not even begun and most of the shopping Graham's mother obtained was from the Co-op in Old Harlow or we would get it from Epping or Bishop's Stortford at the weekend.

On one of our trips to Epping in Graham's old Morris Tourer on a Saturday afternoon, Guy Fawkes' Day in November 1955, Graham's mother asked us to buy her a pound of sausages. We drove up leisurely, window-shopped, bought the sausages and, as it was a very cold and dank late afternoon, started to drive back early, in order to be at mum and dad's house in time for tea. It was twilight and foggy in patches, making Graham, who was always a sensible and careful driver, drive even more carefully than usual. As we left the traffic lights near Old Harlow High Street, we encountered a large pocket of fog. We, therefore, drove extremely slowly. Suddenly, as we approached Harlow Mill, now the Beefeater, we felt a dull thud and saw a large cow mount the bonnet. We stopped dead. There was a whole herd of cows in front of us enveloped in fog trying to cross the road, mixed up with slowly moving traffic. We both felt sick. The poor injured cow was lying in the road in front of us and there was the possibility of more poor cows suffering the same fate, if we did nothing to prevent the rest of the herd following her example.

Graham hurried out of the car, asked a driver who was coming from the opposite direction to telephone the Police and then stood in the road directing the traffic and trying to get what seemed to me like hundreds of cows out of the road. I was panic-stricken. As we did not see the cows because of the thick pocket of fog, so I felt other drivers would not be able to see Graham. I visualised him mounting another car's bonnet and hitting the windscreen. Therefore, I implored him to get back in the car, in order not to court danger and death, or at least serious injury. Reluctantly, he agreed.

After collecting our thoughts, we drove the car into the Harlow Mill car park and went inside to wait for the Police to come. I had always wanted to go to the Harlow Mill restaurant, as it had a very good reputation, but had never imagined sitting in the reception tired, cold and hungry, waiting for the Police. Eventually, after what seemed an eternity, they arrived and took statements. They were followed by the vet, who had to shoot the poor cow, as it was so badly injured

Bedraggled and still suffering from shock, we drove up the half a mile to mum and dad's house in Redricks Lane, to arrive almost at their bedtime, at around 10 pm, to be greeted by mum with: "We've had our tea. We don't need the sausages now. You are late! I expect you went to the cinema, that's why you are late."

We explained the real reason and were given a lot of sympathy, as well as a hot drink and something to eat.

I could never understand why Graham lost his no claim bonus over this incident. No one could have seen a cow cross a busy road in thick fog. Surely, it is the farmer who let his herd cross a main road in foggy weather who should have been penalised.

When I read the above to Graham, he reminded me that the farmer also claimed the cost of the cow, which the Insurance Company had to settle!

CHAPTER 7
Marriage And Our Life Together

The week after we came back from Bournemouth, Graham contacted his best friend Maurice's mother, Mrs Cray, who lived only a few doors away from his parents and worked in Ashwell's, the jewellers in Bishop's Stortford, in order that we may choose a ring. We chose a solitaire, which Mrs Cray obtained for us at a special price of £11 (four weeks' salary) and I was so proud when Graham put it on my finger. Needless to say I am just as proud wearing it today, over 49 years later.

The next event we had to plan, of course, was our wedding. We decided that we would get married on 7 July 1956 and Graham asked Ivan to be his best man. Graham's brother, Sidney was in the Army in Cyprus at that time and, although we hoped he would be allowed to come, we could not be absolutely sure.

Mama booked Wolf's Restaurant near Sidcup Station and we booked the wedding at the Anglican Church of Holy Trinity in Station Road, Father Groom to officiate.

Most of my friends were taller than me, which would not have been in order for bridesmaids. Therefore, I was very pleased when Pamela accepted to be Matron of Honour at our wedding.

The biggest worry now was where would we live after the wedding. As the time drew nearer, we almost became panic-stricken. Harlow New Town, as it was then known, because of its small size at the time only accepted people for rehousing from overcrowded London areas. Then we had a stroke of luck.

Mrs Cray heard from Ashwell's that there could be a flat available above their proposed new shop in the High Street, if we would care to decorate it and make a small kitchen out of the landing. We jumped at the chance. Nothing could be settled, however, until after the wedding, as Ashwell's were still negotiating the purchase of the building.

During the next few months I was preoccupied with everything to do with the wedding but, in the first instance, with the design of my wedding dress. Do I buy a ready made dress or do I have one made by a dressmaker, who used to work at Court? What neckline should I have? What material? I doodled innumerable necklines on every available scrap of paper, changing my mind like the proverbial English weather.

Incidentally, my mother could never get over the fact that in England every conversation, when meeting someone in the street, always began with a reference to the weather and her favourite joke was:

Foreigner: "I love England, but I don't particularly like your English weather."

Londoner: "Don't worry, mate! Just wait a minute and we'll change it for you."

Eventually, I walked through John Lewis' in Oxford Street, glancing at materials, when my eyes fell on a beautiful, creamy white, heavy satin brocade, embossed with a pattern of lilies of the valley, my favourite flowers and scent and my mind was made up. I remembered at the same time a lovely Vogue dress pattern I had bought just in case.

Our wedding day, 7 July 1956

The material in my bag, I rushed to catch my train home. Whom should I meet when changing trains at London Bridge, but Reg. Would I, please, go back to him? Did I still love Graham and was I still going out with him?

"Yes! A thousand times, yes, to the last question! In fact, we are getting married in July and I've just bought the material for my wedding dress." His parting shot: "I hope you don't use it!", made me realise what a lucky escape I had had.

At that time, when a female employee of the bank married, she had to leave her job. It seems almost laughable now! However, I knew also that it would not be practical for me to travel up to town to work after the wedding and, therefore, I looked for a local job. I had been very happy in the bank and was a little reluctant to leave, after seven years. I had known no other employment, although I was lucky enough to be adaptable. If nothing else good came out of my experience in life, my adaptability has certainly stood me in good stead.

As the evening of my departure loomed near, I realised what a wrench it would be to leave the bank, but I had so much to look forward to.

Amid speeches and farewells, I was presented with a beautiful dinner service from Heal's and wished good luck. Several of my friends from the bank came to our wedding, particularly Gladys and Eva, who had watched me mature and seen me through many ups and downs, including an office romance, which was a non event on my part, but highly amusing for my colleagues. I liked the person concerned, who told me how much he liked, fancied and admired me and asked me out frequently, but I could not envisage going out with him, whereas my friends thought he would be a perfect match for me. In order to spare his blushes, I am not naming him.

We had no money with which to get married, but we both had

jobs and we were not afraid of hard work. I had managed to get a job as a secretary to one of the management team at STC Rectifiers in Harlow and Graham's auntie Lily, a widow, had promised us a roof over our head in the form of a bedroom, until our little flat in the High Street was ready.

We had no money for a honeymoon and Graham needed a new suit for the wedding. We wondered what to do and finally Graham decided to sell his beloved Morris 8, soft-top, despite the fact that it meant a lot to him. We also realised that if we kept it, we would not be able to afford to run it. Thus, we managed to book a week's honeymoon in Torquay.

Graham spent the night before the wedding at my friend, June's house, and was collected by Ivan early in the morning, in order to go for a stroll through the park. The weather was so beautiful that they spent some time, fully dressed, sunbathing on a bench in the park, feeling completely relaxed, waiting for 12.30 to come. I seemed to have been just as relaxed in my preparations, as I remember thinking that we should have arranged the wedding for mid-morning rather than have to wait so long for the appointed hour to come.

At last the time arrived and we were standing side by side in church, gazing at each other, my hand tightly clasped in that of the man about to become my husband. Father Groom gave us a very inspired little sermon, emphasising that we must always try to please one another. Whilst he was giving us this advice, I suddenly thought and began to worry that Graham loved Yorkshire puddings, yet I forgot to ask mama how to make them! Will it mean that our marriage will collapse, as I could not please my husband in the kitchen? It was too late now to learn how to cook a Yorkshire pudding, as we were going straight to Harlow after our honeymoon!

Although Graham had many relations and friends at the wedding, I was sorry his old grandfather would not come, asKent seemed almost abroad to him, who lived all his life in Essex. However,

Graham and I were always very fond of him and, after we were married he often used to come to us for meals, especially at Christmas time, until he died aged 87. He was a wonderful old man, who cycled to work on farms almost till the day he died.

What excitement we felt and caused when we left on the first leg of our journey by car to London!

Our friends, Mr and Mrs Alan Thomas - Alan was our dentist and friend in Sidcup - promised to drive us in their Jaguar Mark VII, which was the height of luxury to us. We just reached Paddington Station in time to catch the train to Torquay. As we left the restaurant to get into the car, we noticed that the film showing at the cinema next door was "A Walk into Paradise" and felt it was a good omen.

The Forest Hotel, Torquay, was a very pleasant, medium-priced place, just out of town. This did not matter, as the hotel provided transport to and from Torquay harbour in a Dormobile. We made friends with a charming couple, Mr and Mrs Field, but did not tell them that we were on our honeymoon. However, when the proofs of our wedding photographs arrived midweek, we were so thrilled with them that we had to tell them the truth and show off the photographs. We corresponded with them for years, long after Mr Field had died and Mrs Field moved away.

On our return we began the busiest time of our lives. We slept and had breakfast at auntie Lily's, went to work our separate ways, then met up for our evening meal at Graham's parents' house in Redricks Lane, Harlow. As soon as we had eaten, we would rush off to No 1 High Street in Old Harlow, in order to do some painting and decorating in our little flat, which slowly began looking habitable. It consisted now of two large rooms, bathroom, toilet, small kitchen on the landing and two rooms in the attic, but more about these later. At weekends, of course, we spent all our time working on the flat.

When I told Graham that when I left the bank they credited my account with the sum of £280, representing my dowry, he said I must keep that money purely for my use and he would not touch it. I told him it would be ridiculous for us both not to use it for purchasing essential furniture and requirements for our first home. After the first and only argument I remember us having in the run up to and after our marriage, until we had children (!), and even then nothing serious, he capitulated and allowed me to use the money to buy two kitchen stools, a length of second hand stair-carpet and a few other essentials.

We actually moved into the flat on 1 September, exhausted from our busy lifestyle of the last six weeks. I remember it was a very wet day, with hardly a minute without rainfall. As all our clothes were sopping wet, I had to rush to the local hardware shop to buy a clothes airer. When I came back with a new stove-enamelled type and told my parents-in-law and Graham that it cost thirty shillings - a lot of money then - they were amazed at the expense. However, it is still in hard use nearly fifty years later, so it was a bargain in disguise.

For the first time in my life I was unhappy at work. My boss and I seemed to be compatible on the surface, but there appeared to be some dissatisfaction on both of our sides and, therefore, I decided to call it a day. In retrospect I discovered that he only gave me the job, in order to boast that his secretary could speak several languages and was very well qualified.

Leaving my job at STC was the best decision I ever made, as I walked into a job where I could not have been happier and I could, therefore, forget the other one completely and erase the last two months from my memory.

I became secretary and PA to the Technical Director of Key Glassworks, just across the road from STC Rectifiers. My boss, Mr Alfred Moorshead, was the perfect boss and, although I worked for other people as well, such as the Chief Engineer, Chief Chemist, etc, as I had time to spare, he was always very appreciative of any effort on my part. I enjoyed being in my little office in the front of the building, almost overlooking the building where I was so unhappy.

Our life at the flat settled into a happy, busy and uneventful existence, except for one night during the second week of our residence. We were lying in bed talking, when I suddenly heard footsteps walking across the ceiling. Graham too, had heard them, but assured me that, as most of these very old houses were made of lath and plaster, if someone walked at the end of the High Street, then it could echo on to our ceiling. As I believed these were ghostly footsteps, I took some convincing, but apparently accepted his explanation.

Nevertheless, I decided I would never be in the flat on my own. When Graham attended evening classes for his Bankers' Institute examinations, I would also go to whatever was available on the same night at Mark Hall Evening Institute. The only subject available was woodwork, so that is what I took up. I was by no means the only female student and in my first year made a standard lamp and a very large tray to accommodate six cups, saucers and tea plates, among other things, at the same time. Many years later, long after we had moved away, Graham confessed that he had made up the lath and plaster story on the spur of the moment and he, too, believed the place was haunted.

We had our first party in that flat: housewarming. I still recall the excitement I felt when I prepared all the food and punch in that tiny kitchen. Had we invited all the people who had helped us get started or did we leave someone out? Had we enough food? Did everyone eat potato salad, etc, etc?

Gradually, the little flat was buzzing with noise. Graham's parents, auntie Lily, auntie Connie, Sue, Ivan, all arrived. Graham's best friend, Maurice, had borrowed an office dictating machine, which we used as a tape recorder and recorded several spoof Goon type dialogues which, when played back at around 3 am sounded quite funny. In those far off days of course, cassette players had not been invented.

I remember we finally said goodbye to our last guests, at least those who lived locally and were not staying the night, at about 5 am. Several people slept on mattresses on the floor in the lounge, while Ivan slept partly on the landing, partly in the kitchenette, in a sleeping bag.

It seemed as if we had just fallen into a deep sleep, when we woke up to the clatter of teacups and found Ivan, ever thoughtful, dangling cups of tea above our heads. He said he woke up with his head under the sink and the sight of all those dirty dishes spurred him into action. He thought if he brought us a cup of tea in bed, we would get up and deal with the dishes. The trouble was that he had made the tea by pouring hot tap water on to cold tealeaves left in the pot the night before!

The tea served its purpose. We rose quickly to start washing up and clearing the debris, then served breakfast to all the people who had stayed the night. By the evening the flat was tidy again and no-one would have guessed that there had been a riotous party the night before.

Whilst living in the High Street, we had our name down for a Harlow Development Corporation flat for many months and had almost forgotten that fact when, out of the blue, we had a letter from them, offering us 54 Northbrooks, a ground floor corner maisonette, with a large garden in a new block of maisonettes, very near the Town Centre. We found the letter when we came home from work, ready to leave the next day for a week's holiday in Ostend, Belgium where we were going to celebrate our first wedding anniversary. We did not know what else to do, but to cycle to see it through the window, as the Housing Office was closed for the weekend. We had to let the Corporation know by Monday if we wanted it.

While we were at the maisonette, peering through the windows, a charming couple, Mary and Stan, were tinkering with their motorbike in the unmade road nearby. They introduced themselves to us and offered to show us round their maisonette, which was directly above the one offered to us. We jumped at the chance and thus began another friendship, which has lasted nearly fifty years.

As soon as we saw Mary and Stan's maisonette, we realised how lucky we were to be offered the same, especially as ours had French windows opening onto a large garden. We, therefore, wrote a letter to the Corporation accepting their offer, put it through their letterbox and departed for Ostend.

We had a wonderful holiday that year, most of it spent on the beautiful Belgian beaches. In the evenings we went on many excursions, but we celebrated our first wedding anniversary at the casino with a superb meal and a glass of champagne. Graham gave me an eternity ring and we had no care in the world. We gave each other cards saying 'To the next 87 years!' We felt secure in our love and, being healthy and happy, could not envisage anything but joy stretching before us in our life together. I also remember fleetingly recalling my thoughts a year previously, when in my mind I likened marriage to a raffle and hoped that both Graham and I had drawn the identical winning number and that we would make each other happy. By now I knew that we were so lucky to have met each other and married.

Every so-called authority on marriage always seems to state emphatically that the first year is the hardest, but I can neither agree not believe that it presents any hardship at all. I would like to be able to say that we worked particularly hard during that first year on establishing a firm foundation for our partnership, adapting to each other's likes, dislikes and foibles, giving and taking in equal measure. However, we did not consciously work at it at all, in order to make our marriage work; we just happily sailed through that year, despite the hard physical work of getting the flat ready, holding down full time jobs and getting used to considering another person's opinion on every subject of importance or every decision which had to be taken. For us, the words of the Beatles' song, as yet unwritten, certainly seemed to come true: "All you need is love . . ."

On our return from holiday, we moved into 54 Northbrooks, where we stayed for nearly five years. Within a few days of our moving in, our next-door neighbours arrived, with a three week old baby, Carol, who was very sweet and beautiful. The wheel has turned full circle twice, for recently I learnt that Carol's son, has become a father to a baby girl.

Another pleasant couple, Jim and Hazel, with baby son, Ian, moved in, followed by Dorothy, Bryan and baby Anne, in the flat next door to Hazel and Jim. All these neighbours, including Mary and Stan above us formed the nucleus of our friends at that time. Mary and Stan and Graham and I were the only ones without children. We, therefore, made a great fuss of the little ones, but I did not realise that I was spoiling them, until Carol came in one morning and said: "I would like, umm . . . sorry, auntie, let me think what I would like today . . . !" I knew then that I had to limit my largesse and confine it to occasional sweets or toys.

We used to celebrate all festive occasions together, mostly because it was difficult for the others to get out without the children. Although we did not live in each other's pockets, whenever anyone needed a friend, needed to celebrate good news or someone with whom to commiserate, we were all eager to participate. The night Dorothy went into hospital to have her second child, Paul, for example, little Anne spent the night in my bed, while Graham drove Dorothy to hospital, as Bryan was at sea at the time; he was in the Navy. On the other hand, when I was expecting our first baby, Neil, Dorothy came to keep me company as much as she could, when I was confined to bed trying not to have a miscarriage. She is one of Neil's Godmothers.

We used to have a party always on Boxing night, while Mary and Stan usually had one on New Year's Eve. The reason we had a Boxing Day party was unusual: Leslie always used to have 1kg of caviar sent to him from Iran every Christmas, which had to be eaten pretty quickly, as it would go off. We would all have some for tea on Christmas night in Sidcup, if we were there and then Leslie gave us what was left to bring home to Harlow, invite all the neighbours and feast on brown toast and caviar. Although none of us was rich, we all soon developed the taste for caviar and really looked forward to our unusual Boxing Day tea.

FOOD OF THE GODS

Caviar! Sturgeons' eggs!
Glistening in a heap
on a dainty dish
of blue and white porcelain,
ready to be piled
on to thin triangless
of brown bread.
A feast every Christmas:
a kilo, courtesy of a firm
in far off Iran;
tiny ball bearings
in a suspension of grease.
Never knew we had so many friends
in our tiny council maisonette.
No substitute lumpfish roe then -
no better feast.
I could live on this
For every meal!..

CHAPTER 8
Nothing But Troubles Ahead, Or Were They Just Minor Obstacles?

We had a week's holiday in 1959 in St Ives, Cornwall at a guesthouse on the sea front, where everyone thought we were on our honeymoon. We enjoyed ourselves swimming, walking and a little mild rock climbing. On our return, I complained of a slight pain in my left leg and back, which gradually worsened. I was convinced that the pain was due to a fall on the rocks in Cornwall and the subsequent bruising. However, as it did not clear up, I thought it prudent to go to the doctor and ask for an X-ray, in case I had broken something.

I found myself at Rye Street Hospital, Bishop's Stortford, facing Dr C on a certain morning, with bright sunrays fighting their way through to penetrate the X-ray photographs of my spine on the clinical stand. My mother-in-law, who was a retired district nurse and a part time staff nurse during the war at Rye Street, had advised me to ask for that hospital and Dr C, in particular, as she still believed them to be the best in the district.

Dr C: "Well, Mrs Peacock, this is extremely serious. You had a broken spine. some time in the past, caused by poor diet or starvation. Please get on the couch and I will examine you."

Me: "This is not possible, although I did starve and have a poor diet in my teens. Could these be someone else's X-rays? I only had a slight fall on the rocks in Cornwall on holiday!"

Dr C: "These are definitely your X-rays. Let's see now (motioning me to the examination couch)."

I lay down and submitted myself to the examination. On completion, I jumped down off the couch.

Dr C: "Look at that, nurse, isn't it remarkable? She jumped down like a two year old! Do you manage to do any of your housework, Mrs Peacock? Do you suffer from chronic backache?"

Me: "I do all my housework and have a full time job as secretary to the Technical Director of a large Company in Harlow. I cycle to and from work every day and I have less backache than most housewives."

Dr C: "Have you any children?"

Me: "No, but we would like some soon and we are going to try soon for a baby."

Dr C: "That is out of the question at the moment. Your spine could never support a pregnancy. Just as well you have no children, as you will be able to be admitted quickly and I will do a bone graft on your spine. You will be in hospital no longer than six months."

Me: "Before I agree, could I, please, speak to my husband on the telephone?"

I then left the room in a trance and walked out of the hospital across the road to the telephone kiosk. My whole world seemed to be lying in ruins at my feet: my job, hoped for family, Graham's and my life together. Six months in hospital! That is if the operation was successful. What if it was not. I had read somewhere that it was very dangerous to tamper with the spinal column, because of the possibility of injuring the spinal cord.

I had walked into the hospital a bright, self-confident young woman expecting to be told, perhaps, to rest for a week or two, in order to let some lightly bruised bones recover, yet here I was walking out of it only half an hour later a shattered, hopeless woman, feeling distinctly middle aged at 28. Amid tears of disbelief and worry, I poured the contents of Dr Coleman's and my interchange into the earpiece. Incredulous, Graham just whispered: "Don't worry, darling, we'll sort this out. Don't agree to anything until we have had a chance to confirm all this."

How lucky I was to have met and married someone like Graham, who has always been able to think rationally, even in times of stress, and be very supportive. In retrospect, due to my many illnesses and crises, he has now had plenty of practice!

Very faintly reassured, I returned to the consulting room, where Dr C agreed to leave things as they were for the moment, but sent me for a blood test. When the result of the blood test was known, he said, he would send for me.

The next few weeks passed very slowly. I enjoyed my work, even though I had to work hard in my office during the day. At least it left me with little time to worry about my spine. However, my nights were full of nightmares, even during my waking hours in the evenings. I felt as if my whole body consisted of a walking stick: the crook was my head and the rod my body. I was only conscious of my brain and spine.

Weeks went by and I heard nothing from the hospital. Whilst at work one day, I consulted our Works doctor, a kindly gentleman, Dr B, with whom my mother-in-law once worked. I knew that he was fond of the family and would tell me the truth, whether I needed a bone graft or not and what spondylitis, for that was the name given to my condition by Dr C, meant. He explained it all in graphic and easily understood terms: the discovery of my illness was equivalent to discovering that there was a hole in the ground on the way to work for someone. He passed this way often, but never saw it before. However, now that he had discovered it, he would always be careful to avoid it. Now that the doctor had discovered the weakness in my spinal column, the hospital would always keep a check on me.

To this day, I have never had the result of that blood test or heard another word from the hospital. However, the anguish that interview caused me remained for months, almost years, with me. No explanation was ever given. I am sure, though and was assured by the hospital, that the X-rays were mine, for how many English people would have starved and suffered similar deprivation during their teens. Maybe God had answered once again my fervent prayers and cured me?

During spring of 1960 we bought a tiny caravan, a Berkeley Caravette, intent on spending our summer holiday touring Devon and Cornwall. The inside area of the tiny caravan was 6 ft x 4 ft and it was about 4 ft high. Therefore, one could either sleep in it or eat in it, but never both at the same time; ie, the bed folded into a settee when not in use and one could sit, but not stand inside. The back of the caravan lifted up to expose the kitchen: a primus stove and two saucepans! When I compare that with our present modern motor caravan, I cannot believe how happy we were with such basic facilities. Although I have always enjoyed caravanning, I could never get on with camping. At least, even in this little apology for a caravan, if it rained we could hide ourselves in the dry on the settee, even if we could not stand up.

We looked forward to going on holiday, but in June I thought that I had become pregnant and jubilantly hurried to the doctor for confirmation. He said it would be better if he did not examine me at that time and told me to return in about a month. Meanwhile, I visited the Family Planning Association in London twice, each time taking a specimen with me and asked them to test it for pregnancy. Each test was negative. I believed at the time that the test was conclusive, but apparently it was not. When I returned to the doctor, he examined me and he, too, confirmed that he did not think I was pregnant. Therefore, he advised us to go away in our little caravan and forget all about it. We followed his advice and decided that it would be silly to postpone a well-earned holiday for a whim.

We enjoyed our holiday immensely and found many seaside and farm sites where, because of its rarity value and cuteness, we attracted friends at every site where we stopped. People did not believe that we could sleep in such a small van; they thought that we just used it for picnicking, if it rained. The only thing that marred our holiday was the fact that I began bleeding slightly.

On our return, I again went to Dr M, to say that I thought I might be having a threatened miscarriage, when he pooh-poohed the idea.

We looked forward to Ivan and Jenny's wedding on 17 September, when Graham was going to be their best man. The wedding was beautiful in a little church in Chislehurst. Jenny looked exquisite and I was very proud of Graham when, in his speech, he said he hoped "Ivan and Jenny would be as lucky and happy in their marriage as my wife and I are in ours."

That evening, after the reception, we went back with mama and Leslie to their house, but I was very restless and had a bad backache. We, therefore, drove home to our maisonette and went straight to bed. Within an hour I had to wake Graham, as I was haemorrhaging. He telephoned for Dr M who, as soon as he arrived, examined me and said: "Yes, Mrs Peacock, you were pregnant after all, but now you are having a miscarriage. At least now you know you can become pregnant." This was like telling a chef, who had slaved over a hot stove preparing a delicious meal for hours, that there had been a surge in electricity and his meal was burnt to a cinder: "Never mind, at least you knew how to use the right ingredients and how to cook the dishes."

Needless to say, I was very upset and felt that I could have, perhaps, saved a threatened miscarriage, had I followed my own instincts and taken it easy.

The ambulance came to take me to Herts and Essex hospital in Bishop's Stortford - the Princess Alexandra Hospital in Harlow was not even started then. I lost our baby at, apparently, three or four months' pregnancy and was desolate. I believed then that I could never love a baby as much as I had loved this one, but luckily this feeling passed several months later. The worst moment came when I returned home, physically quite well, to find that my body had still not adjusted to losing the baby, as milk came out of my nipples. I spent a week at home convalescing, before returning to work, doing a lot of embroidery, which seemed to be therapeutic.

As I was being driven to the hospital by ambulance, someone told me that I was not the only one to be rushed through the night, to be admitted as an emergency, in the throes of a miscarriage. Therefore, throughout the night I prayed both for the safety of our baby and that of the unknown mother and baby who were in the same predicament. When, in the morning, I lost my baby, I still prayed that the other girl would keep hers. One can imagine, therefore, my feelings when, a day or two later, I met the other girl and found that she lost the baby she was carrying and that she was trying to get rid of it anyway, as she already had two young children and a job which she would have had to give up!

As we were now not going to have a baby immediately, Graham and I decided that we would be able to afford to buy a television instead and that is how we became the proud possessors of our first television set. The luxury of not having to go, rain or shine, to Graham's parents to see a programme we wanted to watch occasionally was very much appreciated.

We were told to wait two to three months before we tried to conceive another baby and we did as we were told. However, when I then immediately became pregnant, as planned, and followed this with another threatened miscarriage, our new doctor, Dr Mildred Gordon, advised me to stay in bed for four weeks. I shall never forget the day she examined me at the end of that time and said I was still pregnant and it looked as if everything might be all right this time.

The time in bed passed quickly. I was never short of visitors, as neighbours would often pop in. I remember there were twelve of them sitting round my bed watching television, when the Allison Brothers won the Eurovision song contest with their song 'Are you sure?' in the spring of 1961.

Once I was up, I returned to work. It really was exceptionally good of Key Glass, but my boss, Mr Moorshead particularly, to let me have time off, then come back for a little while, prior to leaving to have a baby. My eventual departure from the firm was very appropriate, on 21 June 1961, as my boss was also retiring that day to his new house in Rustington. I was very impressed with my Testimonial from him stating that he "thoroughly recommended me for any position I would care to apply".

I enjoyed my pregnancy very much, despite the early fears of losing the baby and despite a touch of high blood pressure and hygromnia (water on the tummy), towards the end. Dr Gordon thought I would probably need a Caesarean section, as my pelvis was small, although when I visited the hospital, Dr Samson said this would not be necessary.

The baby was due on 26 August but, as there was no sign of labour by the second week in September, I was taken into hospital. Dr Samson was on holiday and I, together with several others, waited and eventually had my water broken, in order that labour would start.

Apprehensive, yet thrilled, I timed the first labour pains twenty-four hours later, on Saturday afternoon, 16 September, with Graham holding my hand. At last we would have a baby!

To cut a long story, or should I say labour short, after trying to deliver the baby normally, throughout most of Sunday, then with forceps, Dr Samson said: "You'll get your wish, Mrs Peacock. I will have to do a Caesar after all."

The truth was, having returned from holiday he had had to do seven Caesars all lined up for him that weekend and apparently he did not want to do what might have been an unnecessary one, so I heard afterwards.

I surprised even myself with my clear reply: "My wish is to have a baby, Dr Samson. How I have it, I don't care!"

By this time it was the visiting hour on Sunday afternoon, 17 September, exactly a year to the minute of Ivan and Jenny's wedding and exactly a year, of course, to the day when I had my miscarriage, which resulted in the loss of the first baby we had longed for.

The first Graham knew of what was happening, was when he saw the surgical team scrub up and come through wearing green surgical boots. All I remember of it was seeing the friendly face of a doctor from our medical practice in Harlow, who had come to act as an emergency anaesthetist, encouraging me to be brave and the terrible feeling of suddenly having to stop pushing, now that the Caesar was imminent, when all I wanted to do was push. And then . . . the blissful coming out of the anaesthetic to see Graham holding my hand and a nurse holding a beautiful baby, with a shock of bright auburn, red gold hair and someone whispering "You have a baby boy."

My first words: " Oh, my uncle Albert", referring to Neil's hair, did not reflect the bursting happiness and pride which I felt, before falling into sleep again and staying sedated for nearly three days and nights, missing the news of Dag Hammarskjold's assassination/death in an aeroplane that week.

I had to stay in hospital nearly three weeks, due to an infection under the scar of the operation, which had to be irrigated with hydrogen peroxide regularly. Apparently, that part of the wound became infected due to the fact that it was neglected over the weekends, when there was not enough staff on duty. Thank God,

MRSA was not rife at that time in hospitals!

Despite valiant efforts to feed Neil myself, both in preparation at home before I had him and whilst still in hospital, he had to be put on National Dried milk. When we returned home, I tried him on other, more expensive foods, but he could not tolerate them. He was a healthy, but 'sicky' baby, who took hours to take a bottle. We used to have a large bowl where 20 - 30 teats with different sized sucking holes floated in Milton. Some were too fast, some too slow, hardly any just right. As my scar had not healed yet, it was a nightmare trying to visit the district nurse for dressing it, in between feeds. I think babies sense inexperience and exploit it to their advantage.

As soon as my scar had healed, mama and Leslie became ill. Mama had had another stroke which, although not life-threatening, this time, had put her in hospital. Leslie, too, was in another hospital, although I can't remember why; probably for another operation to have kidney stones removed. He had already had one of those years ago. At that time, doctors did not try to dissolve the stones or get them to be passed through, if they were not too big, as happens now. Therefore, Graham and I and our new baby, Neil, had to go to stay in mama and Leslie's new house in Chislehurst for the duration of their hospital stays.

Although it was lovely to stay in a beautiful, new and very spacious house, with new furniture and a large garden the size of a park, it was a nightmare trying to keep everything spotless, particularly the settee, with a sicky baby around. Graham, of course, travelled to London to work every day, whilst I seemed to be occupied with giving Neil his bottle most of the day, only to have him bring it up after the feeds, or so it seemed to me. However, he thrived and was a bonny baby. We were quite relieved when we could return home eventually and not just because mama and Leslie were out of hospital and recovering well.

At that time, too, our long search for a house, which was cheap enough for us to buy, came to an end. Towards the end of my pregnancy, we saw some houses being built at Finchmoor in Harlow. We were able to choose one of these, to be known as No 52 and spent many weekends gazing rapturously at mounds of mud and piles of bricks that represented our future home. The houses were to be completed around Christmas, which we felt was a good time, because it gave us roughly three months to get used to the baby and for the baby to get into a routine.

We were proud to start our married life in Harlow Old Town. Together with many residents of nearby places, like Epping and Bishop's Stortford, we believed that it was not so good to live in the New Town. However, as soon as we moved to Harlow New Town, we realised that it is unrivalled in friendliness and helpfulness of the people; it also possessed excellent recreational facilities. Thank goodness that the words Old Town and New Town have now been officially removed and we all live in Harlow. Our Town Centre has had a face-lift - more times than I care to remember - very many new shops have opened and still more are opening at the moment. It would be hard to find a better place for young or old to live in.

The only downside is the much-regretted loss of our Dry Ski Slope, which was one of the best centres of excellence for teaching skiing to able-bodied and disabled skiers. Schools used to send pupils to learn this sport from all over Essex and Hertfordshire, prior to going on snow and Harlow trained more Paralympic skiers than any other slope in the country. It also helped children with cerebral palsy to gain mobility and self-confidence.

While I was in hospital having Neil, I made friends with Margaret, who had a baby, John, in the bed opposite. We discovered that Margaret and her husband, Harold, had also bought a house in Finchmoor and thus began another enduring friendship for both generations, for not only were both sets of parents friends, but Neil and John have been good friends since the cradle. As Margaret, Harold and John moved in before us, they were kind enough to heat our new house for a day or two with electric fires before we moved in, in January 1962, when Neil was three months old.

Again, we were so very lucky with our neighbours, as they all became our very good friends and for most of our stay in Finchmoor we gave a New Year's Eve party for everyone. As we all had babies and young children and not very much money, we could not go out on that evening to celebrate. Not that we particularly wanted to, as we had such good company in convivial surroundings and babysitting was not very available to us at that time. Graham's parents were very good to us and visited us every Saturday afternoon, but they only babysat for us once and mum then told our neighbours that they never went out when their children were young and she did not think it right that we should go either. Therefore, we felt we could never ask them again.

Two of our closest friends at that time were a couple, Sheila and Roy, with baby Stephanie, who was Neil's first girlfriend and who called him 'Nyi-Nyi', firstly because she was so excited when she saw him and, secondly, because she could not say Neil. Sheila and I and the two babies would often have a cup of tea together, which greatly helped us to keep sane, as it seemed that, as young mothers, we felt isolated and very lonely, especially on winter afternoons.

When Sheila and Roy moved to Ampthill, Maureen and Peter, bought their house and, luckily, they, too, became lifelong good friends, especially as they had a son, Trevor, similar in age to Neil.

Whilst I was in hospital after I had Neil, all the other mothers who had had Caesarean births said: "Never again!", but I said that a baby was worth all the pain and would certainly like another. Funnily enough, the most emphatic of the other mothers had another baby by the same means less than two years later!

Before I left hospital, I asked how long we should wait before thinking about having another baby, for I had vowed never to have an only child. At that time, I thought that one had another baby for the sake of the first one, but have since formed the opinion that one has more than one child for one's own sake!

The doctor said that, as my next delivery would definitely be an elective Caesar, it would be a good idea to wait two or three years before embarking on another pregnancy. We, therefore, decided that it would be best to think about it when Neil was around two and a half years old. Luckily, this time (as I put it, it is about time I did something right, as planned), I conceived almost immediately and, despite slight worry that I might have a threatened miscarriage, all went well and I felt marvellous. In fact, never had I felt better.

Neil began playgroup and, although he was extremely happy for the whole of his two years there, he was very upset when he went for his first proper day. We had visited the playgroup together and he appeared to love being with a lot of other children. He loved company and all his life has been very gregarious. However, the first time he and the other children from Finchmoor were waiting with their mothers for the taxi to take them to Kingsmoor House, where the playgroup was situated at that time, he clutched my hand firmly and started to whimper: "Please don't send me, mummy. I will do all your washing up, write all your letters, do anything, but please don't send me!"

I still remember the terrible feeling of guilt as I made him get into the taxi with the other children, but I knew that I had to do it, for his sake.

The next day, of course, he was very eager to go and ever since had been very happy to go to playgroup and, later on, school.

When Neil started playgroup and I was pregnant again, we could, at last, afford to have a telephone and all was well with our world. The telephone was such an important milestone in our lives, because Graham never knew when he would be able to come home and yet could never let me know how late he would be.

This was banking in the pre-computer, Saturday morning working age. I know that in the last few years banks have again started Saturday morning opening, but this time it is purely on a voluntary, very well paid basis, which is a completely different kettle of fish. In those days it was obligatory to work on that day with no extra pay. On twice yearly balance days, at that time, it was de rigeur for him to come home after midnight, to find I had wallpapered a room while he was balancing. One New Year's Eve at Northbrooks, I did just that to the bedroom and, when he came home, I gave him a meal, after which he went to sleep on the settee while I completed the wallpapering job by 4 am and then transferred him to bed. Many times I would cook an elaborate special meal for us for 6.30 pm or 7.00 pm, only to find that, due to an error for which they all had to look in the bank, Graham would come in at 9.00 pm, full of apologies. I knew, therefore, that the telephone was a costly, but necessary expense and was thrilled when we had it installed after so many years.

At the time of my second pregnancy I found that Maureen next door was expecting her second baby too; also, Betty, opposite, was expecting her first. Betty and I became best friends for life. Her baby, Jonathan, and our second baby, Tanja, were almost like brother and sister throughout their early life.

Apart from early bottle-feeding problems, Neil was a very lively, happy, intelligent and generous child. He talked very early. We have a tape of him saying 'Hello' at four months. When he was a little older, he was always asking me when we would have a baby. Also preserved on tape, we asked him

"What would you like most, Neil?"

"A baby, please."

"A baby brother or a baby sister, Neil?"

"Just a baby!"

Neil wanted and needed a bicycle around the time when I was due to go into hospital to have the baby and we decided to buy him one as a present from the baby when I came out, so that he would not be jealous of the new baby, but love it. There was a stall in the market at that time selling tricycles and bicycles. I took him to try some for size. He heard me talking to the lady proprietor and when we came away he put his arms round me, kissed the bump that was my stomach and said: "Thank you, baby!"

Compared with my first pregnancy, my second was a copybook one: healthy, easy, uneventful and completely unmarked by worry. The baby was due in April, we thought. I was to go in on Easter Monday, 19 April 1965 to have an elective Caesar the following day. Graham had his fortnight's holiday booked to look after Neil while I was in hospital. Our new hospital in Harlow, The Princess Alexandra, had just been completed and had started taking in patients at the beginning of April. I wondered if mine was going to be the first Caesar to be performed there in the new Maternity Unit, curiously enough named Samson Unit, after the doctor who performed my first. In actual fact, mine turned out to be the second Caesar.

We had a wonderful Easter Sunday, full of joyful expectancy, revelling in Neil's Easter eggs, rabbits and toys. The Easter Monday that year was a typical, changeable April day. Graham and Neil took me into hospital in bright sunlight at around 11 o'clock in the morning and I remember looking out of the window a few minutes later to see thick flakes of snow falling outside and the sky darkened, as if someone had turned the light off in a planetarium.

I was originally promised the Caesar for the next day, but when I talked to the doctor on duty, he said that, as the surgeon was not coming back from holiday until the following day, he could not perform it then, but leave it for the day after. This, obviously, was wasting a day from my point of view, as it was wasting a day of Graham's holiday and prolonging my absence from him and Neil unnecessarily, so I argued. Eventually, they suggested that if they could get in touch with the consultant surgeon to obtain his permission, the young Indian woman surgeon, Dr Inamdar, would perform the operation on Tuesday morning.

And so it was to be. The night before the operation I was persuaded to have the only sleeping pill I had ever taken and I had the most awful night's sleep ever. It was full of hammers banging in my head, waking, walking round empty corridors, interspersed with fitful sleeping. I was glad when the morning came and the doctor informed me that they had managed to speak to the consultant, who had given permission for Dr Inamdar to perform the Caesar.

I was not afraid of the operation for, after all, what is a little post-operative wind pain, compared with the reciprocal love flowing between a mother and her baby, even if the baby's is only cupboard love, at first! Childbirth, whatever its form, straightforward labour or Caesarean, is a most satisfying experience, because there is usually something beautiful to show for the effort!

Leaving the ward just before ten in the morning, the last thing I remember as I was entering the operating theatre were the following thoughts: we have a definite name for a girl, Tanja Janet Elvira (the last two names being our mothers' names), but, supposing it's a boy!. Ah, well, we'll call him Paul. Paul Peacock. It seemed to scan well.

I also remembered that throughout my first proper pregnancy we had been so preoccupied with names, just like my preoccupation with wedding dress necklines before our wedding. We believed that boys liked the more ordinary, manly names, while girls liked unusual ones. Tanja, although extremely popular in the last thirty or so years spelt differently was quite rare then. Once, when I mentioned to Leslie that we might call a daughter Tatjana, my very favourite girl's name then, he said: "For Goodness' sake, don't, because I'd call her 'Tatty Anna'", so we compromised on Tanja, while Neil was christened Neil Graham Ivan, in case he wanted to be a writer when he grew up and call himself Neil Graham. He was nearly Gregory, as we liked the abbreviated form, Greg. I sometimes wish we had given him a Croatian name, such as Goran or Zoran but, I'm sure he prefers his own!

As I arrived in the anteroom to the operating theatre I asked Dr Inamdar if I could be catheterised after I was under the anaesthetic instead of before, as appeared usual and she readily agreed. She looked so beautiful the day before in her opulent sari and now was clinically dressed like the others, but I still saw the Indian married woman's red mark clearly on her forehead. Her male assistant surgeon and one or two nurses were also Indian. Therefore, they must have felt quite at home when Tanja was born with a red birthmark above her forehead and neonatal jaundice! Oh, Calcutta!

When I came to, Graham was again holding my hand, whispering: "We have a lovely baby girl!"

I kept repeating: "A lovely baby girl! A lovely baby girl!", as if to convince myself that it must be true that we should be so lucky as to have a pigeon pair. Never in my wildest dreams did I think we would have what we had always wanted: a boy and a girl, when only a few years previously we were worried that we would never have a family. The next moment, I surprised even myself, when I heard myself say: "Oh, the pain in my belly! It is just as if someone had cut my stomach open with a bread knife, without an anaesthetic." I had never before used the word 'belly' in my life. A shot of pethidine and the pain was no more.

Before I fell into the arms of sleep with a happy smile on my face, without a single worry, having first caught a glimpse of our beautiful baby daughter, with every ounce of energy I could muster, I telephoned mama to tell her the wonderful news. My voice was still very faint from the operation and I told mama that I would ring off and have a sip of water - nothing else was allowed for a while. Mama was horrified. "My poor darling,", she said. Can you not afford Ribena? I'll send you the money so that Graham can buy you some."

In the morning, of course, there was a £5 note in the post!

I was told that I could have a total of three or five pethidine injections in all. After my second that night I thought I would save some for the awful wind pain I knew would come a couple of days later. However, when I eventually said: "Could I, please, have another of my pethidine injections now?" the nurse laughed kindly and said: "I'm sorry, no! What you don't have in the first two days after the operation, you can't have later!"

Who minds a little wind pain, anyway?

Tanja was an exceptionally good baby. She slept all night and most of the day. I was a little worried that she was too good. However, the hospital assured me that when she was born, they realised she must have been a month premature. Premature babies often slept almost continuously for the full term and she was very healthy and happy, especially as her jaundice disappeared within a few days of her birth.

She was just as good when we returned home, ten days after the operation. I certainly was in much better shape than after my first Caesar and was fully recovered.

In fact, only the day after the operation I made my bed, as the nurses thought I had had a normal delivery. I realise now that this was a little too much, but was not going to argue, I was so happy all was well.

A very important event occurred at the hospital while Tanja and I were its guests. Princess Alexandra came officially to open and name it after herself and, of course, she visited the new Maternity Unit, of which the hospital was justly proud. We all sat in chairs in a semi-circle in the antenatal patients' waiting room, when she came to meet us and shake our hands. She individually asked us questions about our babies and ourselves and actually appeared to listen and be interested in our answers. She always looks beautiful in her photographs, but they do not do justice to her natural beauty, which enchanted us all.

Tanja slept at first all day long in the garden, throughout the beautiful spring of 1965 after we came home. Again, unfortunately, I could not feed my baby, but she progressed well on bottled feeds. We only had two teats at a time floating in Milton - shades of Neil's babyhood and thirty teats. She sucked well and took only a few minutes over a bottle. She was never any trouble. Often second and subsequent children are far happier and easier to bring up, as the parents are much more confident and competent, thus communicating assurance to their babies.

Betty suggested to me one day that it would do me good to go out for a couple of hours and she would look after Tanja, while Neil was at playgroup. Reluctantly, but eagerly, I took her up on her word and caught a bus to the town centre for a break. I went into Wimpy's for a coffee and a hamburger and, when I finished, the waitress asked me what I had. Still up in the clouds of happiness thinking of Tanja, I replied: "A little girl."

She said: "I meant what did you have to eat and drink here?"

When Jonathan and Tanja were very small, they were often together especially as Betty and I, too, spent a lot of time in the summer in each other's gardens. One afternoon she said she would like to return to work and, obviously she would not let anyone else look after Jonathan except me.

After Betty started work as a part time receptionist at a medical practice, I would often take all three children shopping and was proud to take such beautiful and different children out. It seemed funny to see people staring: Neil had bright red gold hair, Tanja's was a shiny dark brown and Jonathan's was platinum golden. I am sure people thought I had had each child by a different father. One day, someone I met asked: "Where does Neil get his red hair from?"

Before I had a chance to answer, Neil replied: "From the milkman." (He had obviously heard the old joke, when I must have said it to someone.)

This time, however, I asked: "Why from the milkman, Neil? The milk is white, isn't it?"

Poor Neil had to admit defeat: "I don't know, mummy."

After Neil started school and Tanja was nearly two, I began to feel unwell. I felt exceptionally tired all the time and had a touch of cystitis with which I went to the doctor. She asked me to take a specimen to the Pathology Laboratory, then come for a prescription to the surgery, when she had the result.

One very early evening, while I was cutting out a dress I was going to make and was feeling as if I was too tired even to finish this simple task, I saw Dr Gordon walking up our front path. I had completely forgotten my Path Lab test and imagined that she was coming to ask Graham for some banking or financial advice. I opened the front door and began: "Hello, Dr Gordon. I'm sorry Graham is not in yet . . ."

"Never mind Graham," she said. "It is you I have come to see. Come and sit down and we'll talk about it."

We went into the lounge, sat down in the armchairs and, when she explained why she had come, I gradually realised that my dream of a happy, hum-drum existence was going to be shattered yet again, and that the seeds of suffering from my youth had once again come to fruition. The legacy of my undernourished and deprived adolescence, when I must have fallen prey to the disease had lain dormant and surfaced, I was told later in hospital.

Dr Gordon told me that instead of doing just an ordinary test for cystitis, the doctor at the Path Lab, who was a student with her at Medical School, was exceptionally conscientious and had tried to grow a TB culture, which took six weeks. Much to his surprise, mine had been positive and Dr Gordon told me that I had renal tuberculosis. She said I would have to go away into a hospital for an indefinite period, anything up to a year probably, but she was not sure, as she was not familiar with the current treatment, which she believed had recently been revolutionised by the discovery of new drugs.

Graham had come home meanwhile and after explaining the position Dr Gordon gave him two tranquillisers for me, in case the shock was too much, but I did not take them.

I was soon to hear from the hospital, as I would first of all have to have an Intravenous Pylogram (IVP) and then, when the result was known, a Retrograde Pylogram, the latter involving anaesthetic and a stay in hospital.

Although I knew that pulmonary tuberculosis was a very serious disease, which was a killer until recently, I had never heard of the renal variation. Also, I suddenly became aware of the Streptomycin and 'PASS' breakthroughs, which revolutionised the treatment of TB and saved thousands of lives. Had I, in fact, had renal TB only about twelve years earlier, my chances of survival would not have been very good. That was when 'PASS' was discovered (1955).

Again, I prayed and was very worried and upset. To have suffered so much already and then to have a dormant TB infection flare up just as our happiness seemed complete, was too much. How was Graham to cope? Every few years from the time he met me, I was in hospital having an anaesthetic and he was pacing outside in a corridor waiting for me to come out of the operating theatre. How would Neil and Tanja manage without their mummy?

A District Nurse visited me every odd day to give me streptomycin injections until I went into hospital for the retrograde pylogram. Both the IVP and now this showed that my left kidney had ceased to function, but the right one was functioning normally. Apparently, when one kidney stops functioning, the other one doubles in size and takes over all the work.

Dr Rhys-Jones, father of Griff, as kindly as he could, advised me that I must not go home, but go into the Honey Lane hospital in Waltham Abbey, for about two months, so that I could be observed, in order to see what drugs suited me and then I could be stabilised. This was a shock, for I began to believe that I would just have to have injections at home. However, I was told that I had no choice, but to go to Honey Lane without even calling at home!

I was completely unprepared for the devastating spectacle that greeted me on my arrival at Honey Lane Hospital, TB ward. Perhaps if I had not come from the new, pristine beauty, attention and comfort of Princess Alexandra Hospital in Harlow, the contrast would not have been quite so obvious.

It was May or June, yet Christmas decorations in all their dusty glory were draped on a telephone trolley in a small room off the ward. There were no locks on the wooden doors of the three toilets, thus giving the inmates no privacy. I use the word 'inmates' advisedly, for one felt much more like an inmate than a patient.

There were about twenty beds in two rows, mostly elderly chest patients, except for three other youngish people, apart from myself. Of these, there was one other renal TB patient, a pregnant girl, and two others, who made my stay bearable. Janet, an artist, who worked in advertising with J Walter Thompson, and Pam, whom I still occasionally see around Harlow and who, like me, is now a grandmother.

The first thing I did, after crying bitterly for a few hours, having been examined by a very pleasant doctor, who could not understand why I was so upset, as his English was not very good, was to take a piece of paper and write ENGAGED/FREE, to hang on to the toilet door. I remember repeating to the doctor, through tears: "How can one hospital have so much and another so little?"

After the first fortnight, thank goodness, I was allowed to go home at weekends, as long as I had my temperature monitored throughout that time and continued my medication. Each patient was given three different types of medicine, including streptomycin injections. It was found that I was allergic to streptomycin and, at first, the nurses made me take two of the same tablets, to make up the deficiency caused by the inability to tolerate strep. I knew that this was dangerous, but they took some convincing; eventually, a doctor convinced them that, if a patient cannot take one drug, one does not automatically double another! Once again I realised that even hospital stays have their hazards.

My next bed neighbour, Janet, was very gifted artistically and, after the initial shock of finding ourselves in the TB ward of a very out of date, poverty stricken hospital, she and I decided that the only way we would make the time pass quickly, would be to keep ourselves as busy as possible. We pestered the very kind occupational therapist to supply us with as much felt as she could lay her hands on and thereafter we flooded Neil, Tanja and all their friends and their friends' friends with glove puppets, Teddy bear brooches, Golly brooches, etc. With regard to the latter, I am glad all this was before the racial discrimination nonsense of PC correctness! I have always found non-white children loved Golly at least as much as white children did.

Our output was enormous, despite the fact that, of course, all the sewing was hand done. At the last count, I think, we had made about

103 glove puppets of felt rabbits and owls. Later I made similar ones in fur over the years to swell the funds of the schools which Neil and Tanja attended. In addition, I knitted Neil and Tanja Shetland pullovers.

The goodies we sent out of the ward had, of course, to be disinfected before the recipients were allowed to have them. I believe they were baked in ovens.

We all felt very sad to be deprived of our families, but Pam felt it most, as her baby, Paul, was only six months old. She was also feeling the most afraid, as her father had died of pulmonary TB and she had had it before. However, all this was before the discovery of the new important drugs, which saved all our lives. She, too, was cured, just like Janet, many others and I.

The bank authorities were very kind to Graham while I was in Honey Lane Hospital. They allowed him to work from 10 am to 4 pm, in order that he may take Neil to school in the morning and be home when he was brought back. Betty, naturally, offered to have Tanja there all the time, but Graham wanted to look after her himself with Neil, except during the day. We, therefore, accepted her kind offer to look after Tanja from 9.30 am to 4.15 pm during the week.

Graham visited me, on average, two or three times per week, as most nights he bathed the children, put them to bed, then collapsed in an armchair. On the nights he visited, the good friends who were our neighbours had a rota of babysitters and we knew our babes were safe.

I did miss the children during the week, but talked to them often on the telephone and, of course, came home to them at weekends. I would usually telephone Betty at about 1 o'clock at lunchtime and speak to Tanja and Jonathan. Tanja used to stick peas all over her face, using mashed potatoes as glue and Betty often made me laugh describing Tanja's decorated face; she has never liked to eat peas -

only recently having started to eat them and then only whilst still frozen.

We were lucky in that both Neil and Tanja were potty trained extremely early, at 12 months of age during the day - they seemed to train themselves - and life was, therefore, much easier for Graham; Tanja was even dry at night at just two. However, every Monday morning, after my weekend at home, Betty would find her behind the television set dirtying her pants; this was, I suppose, in protest at her mother's return to hospital. The rest of the week she was fine.

Most of our friends and parents of our children's friends were fine and very supportive, though some were so afraid that their children could catch TB from Neil and Tanja that they forbade their children from playing with ours. They did not realise that renal TB was different from pulmonary and had it been just as infectious, I would not have been allowed home so regularly. The sad fact is that the person most worried died soon afterwards from cancer and I am lucky still to be alive.

When, after two months, I came home from hospital for good, I was told I would have to go for regular checks to Princess Alexandra Hospital and would have to carry on taking PASS tablets for two years. This I did and felt myself cured at the end of that period. Luckily, I have never minded taking tablets, whatever their size except for unnecessary drugs, but I knew these were essential. As I was used to taking them, I forgot that they were enormous, until one day, just as I was about to take them, a friend said: "Aren't you going to take them out of their little boxes first?" She was quite surprised when she realised they were the actual tablets.

I was told that it would be a good idea in a year or two to have my diseased kidney taken out, as the scarring would make the ureter shrink, which could cause urine to be trapped in the kidney, thus causing high blood pressure, infection or even possible peritonitis, if it burst. For the moment, however, everything was peaceful again and right with our world, except for the perennial money worries which were always with us, though illness seemed to put them in the shade.

As soon as I was well again, when Neil was seven and Tanja three and a half, I wondered what I could do to earn some money at home. And it was not just the money. I felt I was almost a vegetable, not having to think most of the time, automatically taking and fetching Neil to and from school, Tanja to and from playgroup, peeling potatoes, etc, etc. How well I remembered that feeling after my stroke, many years later, when I truly felt like a vegetable, after having to take so many pills to lower my blood pressure.

I then saw two advertisements which interested me. One was for a Sub-editor for a specialised journal: Construction Plant Hire, whose editor lived in Harlow and was a remarkable woman, Mrs Mumby. The other was for a dictaphone-typist to work for the German and French translator of patents, for D Young and Company, a firm of Chartered Patent Agents. I applied for both, had tests and interviews and was offered both jobs.

Each of my home jobs was interesting, different, very stimulating and rewarding, not just in the monetary sense. I enjoyed working for both firms. I felt useful again, a personality in my own right, yet the children did not suffer. I was always there when they came home and they could bring friends home, as I worked mostly in the evenings or while they were out at school or playgroup. Best of all, Graham collaborated with me on the sub-editing job and we both loved doing the work.

Mrs Mumby said she was pleased with the quality of our work and we did more and more for her. Sometimes she would bring the work to us in the evenings and I would have it ready for her early in the mornings. Unfortunately, after a while, she died and the work dried up. The new editor lived too far away to let us do any work for him.

My work for Hilary for she had by now become a good friend, instead of 'the translator for Youngs', continued and I enjoyed being able to type fast from her faultless dictated translations. I also had practice in German and French for, as I listened to the translations and typed them, with my eyes I followed the original patents in their native languages.

When Tanja started school and we needed a little more money, I obtained a part time job as the Manager's secretary at Barclays Bank, Staple Tye, just across the road from us in Finchmoor. I was quite amazed when, having to attend an interview at Barclays Area Office at Cambridge, the interviewer produced my record card and details of employment with the bank twenty years previously. I was very lucky and again enjoyed this work, especially as, at first, I worked mornings only in term time. However much I enjoyed and needed work, I never forgot that my duty was always to be there when the children were not at school.

I still carried on with Young's work at home for a year or so but, when the work in the bank increased, while that for Young's decreased, I gave that up. It was pleasant to work at home, but there is something to be said for going out to work and being able to forget it when one leaves the office to come home, instead of knowing there is always something left pending, awaiting every free moment.

In the spring of 1970, I went for my usual check up to the Chest Clinic at Princess Alexandra hospital. It always seemed funny to me to have to go to the Chest Clinic, when I have never had anything wrong with my chest. However, I can understand that, because tuberculosis is usually connected with the chest, my kidneys belonged to that department. During the interview and examination, Dr Rhys Jones, as kindly as possible, suggested that, as I was obviously in excellent health now, it would be an opportune time to have my left kidney taken out as soon as possible, for the reasons mentioned earlier. I hesitated for a moment, remembering the horror of Leslie's two operations just to remove kidney stones, but was told that nowadays it was just a simple operation: one incision at the side to remove a kidney that was not functioning anyway and I would feel fine forever afterwards, safe in the knowledge that it would cause me no more problems. This, I suppose is what happens to other people when they have a nephrectomy (kidney removal operation), but my problems are never that simple.

When I had been in England several years, we had a letter from auntie Jelka and uncle Emil with some most unexpected and miraculous news: Herta, auntie Olga's daughter and my cousin, who had disappeared when all the rest of her family were sent to the concentration camps, had suddenly arrived from Italy, with a husband and two young boys, Aldo and Sergej. Their story was truly one of the most amazing survivals to have emerged from the Second World War. Somehow, Herta had managed to run away to Italy, where she joined the Italian partisans and met Ivo Raic, originally from Osijek, another young man whose whole family was also annihilated by the Germans at the same time as hers.They fought with the partisans and after they fell in love, she became pregnant with Aldo. When she was giving birth in a house in Italy, in the middle of an air raid, a bomb fell on it and she was trapped by her legs. Ivo managed to free her and carry her to safety. This must have been around 1942. In 1944, their second son, Sergej was born. Both the boys had to have Italian names, in order that the family's roots would not be discovered. Herta and Ivo could not get married until after the war, for the same reason.

Auntie Jelka and uncle Emil were overjoyed that they could offer this last vestige of their family a home and they all lived together for many years. When I heard this news, I realised that it was providential that I did not join auntie Jelka's family when I left the orphanage!

Ivo was highly decorated by Tito for his bravery, for he had transferred eventually to Croatian partisans and was appointed Admiral, which position he held for many years until he retired.

He was a most intelligent, sensitive man, who spoke perfect English, Italian, French, German, Russian, Greek and Spanish, in addition to Croatian, of course. He visited us often in England and made a great fuss of our children. When eventually he and Herta, with the grown up Aldo and Sergej moved to a beautiful flat of their own in Zagreb, we loved visiting them.

While auntie Jelka and uncle Emil were alive, we always had to stay with them for a few days when we came to Croatia and Graham has just reminded me that one year when we, together with Neil and Tanja, were staying with them, we had so much to eat we had to leave the next day. It started with a good breakfast and then a visit to Herta and Ivo's, where we were given delicious cakes and coffee. After coffee, we returned to auntie Jelka's for lunch, consisting of soup, chicken paprikash, potatoes and vegetables, followed by a chocolate torte which, when asked the recipe, revealed to contain 16 eggs. As soon as we finished lunch, uncle Emil told us that his cousin had just had a lovely house built nearby and had invited us to see it. On arrival there, we were ushered in the garden to partake in the most enormous barbeque meal. How we managed to eat anything I will never know.

When we could we made an excuse, praised the house and left, only to be greeted by auntie Jelka on our return with a huge dinner! Hospitality is all very well, but Graham had a word with me and said how much he appreciated my relatives and their generosity, but, please, could we leave for the coast the next day?

No one was prepared for the terrible tragedy which occurred a few months after Ivo retired from his demanding job, which he loved and enjoyed. Apparently, he became depressed and had continuous hallucinations about being hunted by Nazis in concentration camps where his parents died and from whence he escaped. Therefore, one day he climbed one of the tallest buildings in Zagreb and committed suicide. Herta survived, despite her terrible sorrow and the very painful legs which always troubled her - a legacy of the bombed house during Aldo's birth.

Since then, Aldo has married Dubravka and they have a lovely daughter, Vanja, whilst Sergej married Đurđa and they have a handsome son, Nenad. We are quite close to both families, especially now that all the rest of the family is no more and they have all stayed with us several times. When Nenad (Neno) was a teenager, he stayed with us in Harlow and, in order to learn English, he attended the classes for English as a Second Language at St Mark's RC school in Harlow, where I was teaching at the time and made excellent progress. His favourite occupation was visiting the Town Centre McDonald's restaurant as often as possible. Since his graduation, he has found a good job in Zagreb, mainly thanks to his knowledge of English. Vanja, too, has been to London and hopes to come again soon.

At Graham's suggestion, we did leave the next day for the Adriatic Coast, driving our car and caravan through the rugged, stony magnificence of Velebit mountains, to Biograd-na-More, where palm trees proliferate. It was there that Neil and Tanja learnt that if they asked for chocolate ice cream in Croatian, they would always be given either a double portion or the owner would not let them pay. (Jedan čokoladni sladoled, molim! - A chocolate ice cream, please!)

Neil celebrated his ninth birthday there early, with the largest watermelon any of us had ever seen, as I was to have my operation on his actual birthday, 17 September. Tanja was, unfortunately, incubating mumps at the time of my actual operation, according to Mary, who had her for that day and according to whom was "a real poppet". Graham, as usual, was pacing up and down the hospital corridor.

"A simple operation for the removal of a kidney - just one incision at the side. Such a common operation these days", said Dr Rhys-Jones. My only worry was, after reading of numerous hospital blunders all over the country, what if they make a mistake and take the right kidney out? I could not exist with a malfunctioning one!

My case, of course, was different. Apparently, when the surgeon made the incision to take the kidney and ureter out, he - Mr Barron - found such a mess inside, full of lesions, due to the two Caesarean sections, that it would have been impossible to extricate the ureter. Therefore, he had to make another incision where the Caesars were, but far longer. The story goes that so many stitches were needed that "everyone had a go at practising embroidery". In all, 84 stitches for the two operations were needed. The houseman at the time who told me this was an 'Old Boy' of my school, or rather the Boys' equivalent and he was so charming that he helped my recovery a great deal by coming to talk to me whenever he was free. Mr Barron also was wonderful and came to see me patiently explaining what and why they had to do what they did.

It was quite a shock to discover I had had two large operations instead of one medium one, when I came to. The shock must have been even greater for Graham, as he had to pace outside for twice the length of time for one operation, causing twice the worry. I suppose the only benefit of this operation was the fact that, when they examined the excised kidney, they found no vestige of TB. The drugs had wrought their miracle.

If I thought life would be plain sailing after that, I did not communicate this thought. Just as well, though I was not prepared for the shock of the following Sunday afternoon, when death, or at least the possibility of a burst bladder stared me in the face!

When a ureter is removed, it is necessary to remove a small part of the bladder as well. Therefore, a catheter is left with a bag by the side of the bed and the patient is encouraged to drink as much as possible. Whenever I am in hospital and the requests are reasonable, I do everything in my power to comply, as my main object at that time is to get well and back to my family. Therefore, I drank as much fluid as I was asked and then some more for good measure.

I was in a single room throughout my stay this time, not because it was private, but I presume because patients who had undergone serious operations are always left in single rooms, if possible. Everything seemed to progress well and all the nurses congratulated me for being brave and making wonderful progress. Everything, that is, until Sunday. As usual, I drank a pint of water, but there was hardly any liquid in the 'bag'.

"Nurse, I've drank a pint this morning, yet there's hardly anything in the bag."

"That's all right, Mrs Peacock. Don't worry!"

I drank another pint of water, plus some orange squash.

"Nurse, I've drank a lot, but the level in the bag has not altered."

"Don't worry, Mrs Peacock. You are getting neurotic, examining the bag every few seconds!"

"All right! But I am worried. I keep drinking, yet nothing comes out!"

I was feeling very flushed, excited and worried. Perhaps I am being neurotic, worrying about nothing. Perhaps I was just excited because Graham was coming to see me and bringing the children with him. That's what it was! I had seen Graham every day, but had missed seeing the children and, after the worry of the operation, which I had safely overcome, I was looking forward to being 'Mummy' again.

The visiting hour came. Graham walked in all smiles, Tanja and Neil holding his hands. I put on my best welcoming expression then, just before passing out for a second, to the accompaniment of

African drums beating in my head, I managed to whisper: "Please take the children out, darling; I'm sorry, but my bladder is going to burst. Call the nurse and a doctor quickly!"

I came to almost immediately, when the doctor came in with a nurse and changed the catheter. The original one was blocked by a huge blood clot, which came out when the nurse irrigated the bladder with hydrogen peroxide. The doctor then ordered the irrigation every two to three hours for the next 24 hours, day and night, in order to ensure that this dangerous mishap would not happen again. When I saw all the clots that were there each time I was irrigated, I realised how lucky I was to have survived the experience.

Later that evening the young lady doctor, who was on duty that afternoon, paid me a visit and told me how lucky it was that she came in time to save my bladder and me.

I thanked her for her timely intervention. Certainly the pounding in my abdomen and head must have signalled an imminent burst, which she had alleviated.

From then on I made a full recovery, though I have never since felt as fit as I used to feel before I had kidney trouble. Nevertheless, I carried on working at the bank during the school terms, 9 - 3.30 this time and supporting Graham in the new venture which he had undertaken in his spare time.

Graham's father, who was in the building trade, had always told us that if we could obtain a piece of building land, he would like to build us a house. We, therefore, put our name down with Harlow Development Corporation several years previously and promptly forgot all about it. However, suddenly one day we were offered a plot of land at Burnett Park, Harlow, for £2 500. We calculated that, if we did all the work ourselves and subcontracted bricklaying and carpentry, we could build the house of our dreams for the price of our Finchmoor house. We did not realise the superhuman effort this would involve on Graham's part, as by then Dad could not undertake such an assignment.

In actual fact the labour of love, as we like to call Graham's house-building venture, took three years in all from beginning to end. He worked very hard, every weekend, most evenings and many weeks of holiday. During the summers he would take the caravan, the children and me to Cornwall for three weeks to our favourite site at Pentewan, near St Austell, leave us there and come back to Harlow to work on the house, returning to Cornwall for a few days at the end to be with us and bring us all back. The children met their friends from the years before and would be happy and so would I meeting again the same people year after year. We had the sun, the sea and beautiful views and surroundings, fresh fish and our favourite walk around nearby Mevagissey.

Dad told us that the cheapest shape to build would be a rectangular box and we based our design on that. We sketched roughly what we required and then asked an architect to draw us some plans, but told him that we did not need him to supervise the actual building. Therefore, the plans did not cost too much. We needed a detached, four bedroomed house, with a lounge, dining room, study, downstairs toilet, a utility room, kitchen and bathroom. My own only requirement, if possible, was a balcony in front on the first floor. The house also had a double garage, a large semi-circular driveway in the front, with a small lawn, where we eventually planted an ornamental cherry tree and a large garden of 1/3rd acre at the back with a lawn, a rockery, pond and several fruit trees.

When the shell of our new house was completed, we picnicked in the lounge-to-be, conversing with future neighbours, many of whom were busy doing the same things as we were, although some of them had employed builders to do all the work for them.

Once more we were very lucky with our prospective neighbours/friends, this time meeting most of them before we even moved in. One, Paddy, who was going to live two doors away, had something in common with me: she had recently had a kidney removed.

Tanja met her best friend, Lesley, on one of our weekend working visits. They were very similar in temperament, intelligence and interests; they both played several musical instruments well and have remained good friends. Lesley's parents, Brenda and Sydney also became our friends.

Together with Wally, Jean, Peggy and Bob, all these neighbours have remained life long friends, just like those from Northbrooks and Finchmoor.

Graham's father had by then moved out of the district and, although he had promised to build us the house, when we were actually offered the plot, he was unable by then to do more than put in the foundations and the base of the balcony, but he gave us very good advice. In any case, we were grateful to him for giving us the idea that we could accomplish such a feat.

My abiding memory and the only time I physically helped towards the building of the house was when 10 000 bricks arrived one morning early - at about 6 am - in Finchmoor. The lorry driver knocked, told us about the bricks loaded on his lorry, then sat down in his cab. Graham and I put a pair of old gloves on, for the bricks were still hot, and proceeded to unload them, stacking them outside our house. I don't think I had ever worked harder in my life! Eventually, we had to move them all to the new house site the same evening, but they were at least cold by then.

The house was completed and ready in July 1973, when we moved in. Just before, during the building of the house and just after its completion, many sad and happy events in our family occurred. Both pairs of grandparents were extremely happy with their grandchildren and Neil and Tanja adored them all. However, in the space of four years, they were left with just their paternal grandfather, dad. Graham's mother, Grannie to Neil and Tanja, died of cancer after a short illness, in 1969, my mother died of a heart attack and stroke in 1972, whilst Leslie died of a cerebral haemorrhage on holiday in Bulgaria in 1973.

Both Leslie and mama were so looking forward to the completion of our house that I was very sorry mama never saw it finished. Leslie came for the weekend just after we moved in and was thrilled with our effort.

We all felt that at last nothing could go wrong. Although I am always an optimist and believe that after so many tragedies and near tragedies the sun is bound to come out, I do occasionally have cause to remember Betty's philosophy: "Just because so many things have gone wrong and one has suffered misfortune, there is no guarantee that anything else will not go wrong!" How true it unfortunately seems to prove in our family.

Much to our surprise after Mum's death, Dad met and married a wonderful lady of the same age, 63, 'Birdie' Orsman. Her real name was Millicent, but because she loved birds she was always known by her nickname. She was clever, talented, witty - some of her written work could easily have been written by Dorothy Parker - and she was head over heels in love with him. Her love was certainly reciprocated and it was wonderful to see them acting like teenage lovers. They were married at Bishop's Stortford Register Office, with Tanja as bridesmaid. Tanja looked so beautiful that we went straight on to take some photographs in a nearby park to send to Pears' Learning to be a Beautiful Lady competition, no doubt in common with thousands of other beautiful five years olds.

Birdie was an only child of the local bakers in Sawbridgeworth and had stayed at home to look after her aged parents instead of pursuing a University education and a good job. She married for the first time in her forties, but unfortunately found her husband dead in the bath from a heart attack only five years later. She was the leading light in the local amateur Dramatic Society and the Operatic Society and also had many poems and articles published in magazines. She also entered and won numerous competitions; her home and garden were full of her winnings, such as garden furniture, household appliances, furniture, etc, as well as cutlery and crockery.

Having been healthy all her life, Birdie had not seen a doctor or been ill for thirty years, since she consulted him for chicken pox at 33 years of age. What cruel fate then decided that she would have cancer and die such a harrowing death so soon after snatching moments of happiness with Dad? Unfortunately, that is what happened. She started with breast cancer, which was treated, but secondaries had moved into her brain and she died of a brain tumour, not quite realising the end was imminent. We were all around her bed at the time, while she was planning a replacement for her beloved dog, Jonty, who had recently died.

We all, particularly dad, were devastated by Birdie's rapid deterioration and death.

Although I was happy in the bank, I began to have a slight social conscience. I was very surprised and shocked by the quality of education which had been thrust on girls who left local schools to take up positions in offices; their English and quality of typing left a lot to be desired. Unfortunately, at that time, I believed that the reason was bad teaching. Suddenly, I became very keen to train as a teacher and, when qualified, to try my best to turn out better prepared school leavers. I realise now that this was a great over-simplification of the problem. The old adage: You can take a horse to water, but you can't make it drink, I'm afraid still holds good.

It took many years of teaching to realise that most of the blame, if blame is the right word, lies in the modern quest for instant gratification/instant results, on the part of the pupils and the lackadaisical approach to parenthood by some parents, who do not seem to care how their children spend their time, as long as it does not interfere with their own lives. I am still shocked at the freedom given to fifteen and sixteen year old children to stay out all night at parties; parents even provide the youngsters with bottles of gin, whisky and other drinks, in order that they, themselves, can attend other parties or watch horror or blue videos somewhere in the neighbourhood. I believe this also happens to a much younger age group, some of whom wonder round the town late at night and are even found wondering round Soho and other parts of London at around midnight. Don't even poorly educated parents realise that the livers of young people are much more vulnerable and that it takes far less drink for a person under about 25 years of age to become drunk?

The instant results quest syndrome can be perfectly illustrated in the teaching of typewriting or keyboard skills. Girls and boys tackle the subject eagerly at first, thinking that within a few days they would be able to touch type at the rate of at least 50 words per minute. However, when they realise that it require a little perseverance and a lot of skill and enthusiasm on the part of the teacher, they want to fall back on looking at the keys. They usually justify this by saying something like: "Oh, my mum is a secretary and she types by looking at the keys; she's doing all right."

While still working in the bank, I attended evening classes for the City and Guilds Further Education Teacher's Certificate and, when an opportunity came at Stewards Comprehensive School for an Instructor in Commerce, encompassing Office Practice, Typewriting and Shorthand, I leapt at the chance to put into practice what I was learning at evening classes. This would provide me with first hand experience and I could do an In-service Certificate in Education, after completing other qualifications in the evenings and in my spare time.

Neil was by then in the first year at secondary school, while Tanja had moved to Milwards Junior School, which was very near to Burnett Park. Both appeared to be clever, talented and happy in their new schools. They were always very busy with after school activities and had plenty of friends of both sexes. Neil was a very keen football player and had been an eager Cub Scout. He had now moved into Scouts, whose tasks and badges he was fulfilling with equal enthusiasm. He was learning the piano and the guitar. Tanja was just as keen on Brownie and, later, Guide activities and was very musical. From an early age she played the recorder (descant, treble, tenor, bass and sopranino), the clarinet and the piano. She passed Grade VI Clarinet at 11 years of age and Grade V piano and theory.

I left the bank to start teaching at Stewards at Christmas 1973 and was very excited at the prospect. I felt that, with my love for young people and my knowledge and experience of industry and commerce, as well as subject expertise, I had a lot to give and was ideally prepared for the job. At the same time, I started attending another evening class: Royal Society of Arts Typewriting Teacher's Diploma and Shorthand Teacher's Diploma.

In truth, nothing prepared me for my first day's teaching. The previous teacher, a man, had left due to stress and I was thrown in at the deep end. On the first morning I was asked to teach two classes in two separate rooms, commuting constantly between them: one was teaching shorthand, the other typewriting! I will never know how I actually managed it, but I did, without showing my stress. However, at lunchtime, I went into the Staff toilet to have a good cry, where the Head of English, found me and assured me that it would get better. Thankfully, it did and no one should have such a baptism of fire.

After eighteen months of teaching, I wanted to branch out. Therefore, I had a term off without pay, to do the Diploma for the Associateship of the Drama Board in Education, which I enjoyed immensely. It was very hard work, but I felt it extended me as a person tremendously, as well as preparing me to teach Drama in Education. The course consisted of practical drama work at the college and in the Studio at the Harlow Playhouse, several lengthy extended essays on the subject, culminating in a Viva examination at the end and a practical class teaching Drama in Education. I was referred on the first Viva, which I took at Milwards School with a Junior class, but was not too upset, as the failure and referral rates were very high. Fortunately, I took it again a few months later at Stewards School and passed with flying colours.

By 1978, the year that I completed my Certificate in Education and became a fully qualified Secondary School teacher, after five years of part time study at Chelmer Institute of Higher Education and residential blocks at Huddersfield Polytechnic, under the auspices of Leeds University. I obtained Certificates and Diplomas for teaching several subjects and had several years of experience of teaching in three schools. By then I had taught also at Leventhorpe School, Sawbridgeworth and St John's, Epping and felt I could at last relax.

The schools where I had taught simultaneously part time had no full time jobs. Therefore, I looked outside the town. I almost began to despair of ever finding a full time job, now that I was actually qualified, when suddenly I saw an advertisement for a post at King Harold School, Waltham Abbey. I telephoned and, much to my surprise, the school bursar came to collect me the same morning for an interview with the Headmistress and the Head of Commerce Department.

Both the Headmistress, MT and the Head of Department, AD, turned out to be two of the nicest ladies I had ever met. I still think so today, having known them for several years now. In fact, M has retired since. I hope she has the wonderfully busy retirement, which she had planned and so richly deserved.

The job offered to me was that of a fully-fledged commerce teacher, teaching Typewriting and Office Practice to Fourth and Fifth years and RSA Typewriting to the 6th Form. I was very pleased and spent the whole of the summer holiday planning my lessons and looking forward to working with such friendly colleagues. The atmosphere in the staff room was unbelievably friendly.

Although I felt my friends at Stewards and Leventhorpe schools were irreplaceable, it was good to find that my new associates at King Harold School were so friendly, starting with the Deputy Headteacher, down to the youngest probationer. I even managed to get a lift to school every day.

Tanja was by this time at Herts and Essex High School for Girls in Bishop's Stortford, where she was happy and made a lot of new friends, including her clique of six. She was very keen on social service and was always in the forefront of raising money for good causes. One term, I remember, when she instigated a sponsored soft toy making for her class, the total number of toys made was 183, of which she and I made over ninety! The money was divided and sent to two or three charities, one of which was Dr Rob Buckman's Royal Marsden Oncology Club and Tanja treasured his personal letter of encouragement to her.

Neil had been a little difficult, as boys often are from the age of 16 onwards. Most of his friends spent many evenings in pubs and he did not want to be left out although, I believe, he did not drink much. They seemed to be using pubs like we used to use coffee bars.

Many of Neil's friends had all night parties and we seemed to be forever driving round Harlow insisting that he comes home soon after midnight, particularly at the time after he contracted glandular fever in his 'O' level year.

Most of our evenings we were either arguing whether Neil should come home at a respectable time before midnight, or begging his friends to leave our house by about 1 am, so that we could get some sleep. If this is being parents to teenagers, give us babies any time. We never seemed to be in the right! In addition to playing his tapes and records very loudly in his room like other teenagers, he played his electric guitar through a very loud amplifier and the constant beat which came through his floor, ie the kitchen ceiling, was sometimes unbearable. One day, when the constant beat from his bedroom nearly drove me crazy, as it pounded the kitchen ceiling, I rushed upstairs to remonstrate with him, only to find that he had gone out and left the music (!) playing on a loop repeating itself constantly! Although I was cross at the time, it was quite funny.

Neil completed his 'O' levels at Stewards and, despite the minimal amount of study he seemed to put in, had done very well, obtaining all 10 of them with very good grades. However, in order that he might stop staying out so late or having his guitar playing friends here just as late every night, we suggested he might like to go to Davenant Foundation Grammar School for his 'A' levels. He readily agreed and started there in September 1978, settling in very quickly, soon becoming a prefect and a member of the school football team. At the same time, I started teaching at King Harold School.

I enjoyed my first few weeks teaching, especially as the facilities were exceptionally good, although physically I felt a wreck. I just could not understand why I felt so very tired all the time. Perhaps it was my blood pressure. I would go and have it checked.

Dr Hamilton, the doctor who we were lucky enough accepted us when Dr Gordon retired to the Orkneys, took my blood pressure. It was normal. I was obviously worrying about nothing.

On October 12, 1978, school began as usual. Busy classes, but very rewarding work. Even the remedial girl in the fourth year was finally touch-typing. Who says teaching is not satisfying? I recalled how I used to cry in the cloakroom some days at lunchtime in my first term of teaching, both from exhaustion and behaviour of some pupils, until I learnt how to cope with classes. Most of the trouble then was the fact that, as mentioned before, as soon as I started, due to absence of the Head of Department in my first school, I had to cope with two classes at once, separated by a narrow corridor - an almost impossible situation. However, it soon passed and I have loved teaching ever since.

Second period in the afternoon: a library lesson. I arrived in the library to see a fight in the quadrangle, through the library window. Lots of bystanders, while one boy is sitting on top of another, trying to strangle him. I bang on the window: "Stop it!", I shout.

A wag bangs on the outside of the window and shows me his tongue.

"Get off him", I shout, though by the look of it, he has already strangled the other boy. I am obviously mistaken, but for the moment, I am panic-stricken and send for a Senior Master. I settle down to a library lesson, but cannot concentrate.

After afternoon school, the Head of 5th year and I talk things over. I am still very upset, although realise the fight may not have been as serious as I had at first thought. It will be investigated the next day and the culprits punished.

I feel very stressed when I come home and am unable to cope later with Neil and Tanja having a normal brotherly/sisterly argument, which is resolved when Graham comes home.

Peace rules everywhere again. All is right with the world. Neil and Tanja have made it up, they do their homework and go to bed. We kiss them both good night and retire reasonably early.

I woke up at around 4.30 am on Friday, 13 October 1978, certain that I was having a stroke. I don't know why I was so sure, I had certainly never had one before, but the rapid firing of thousands of pins and needles up and down my left arm and leg, followed by immense cramp-like pain, could only signify a stroke to me. I woke Graham and informed him of the fact. "It can't be", he said. "Not now. It is only old people who have strokes."

I was 48 years old. My mother was 70 when she had her first stroke and had been suffering from angina for years. She used to take so many tablets every day I almost convinced myself that, far from improving the angina, they were detrimental to her health. Who knows how a cocktail of drugs taken three times a day interacts? Maybe a certain chemical stops blood clotting or hardening of the arteries, while another combines with it and precipitates a deposit? She was also a heavy smoker, which is often found to be the cause of strokes. I have not smoked a cigarette since my furtive try in the vineyard, when I was ten. In fact, doctors told me later in hospital that, had I been a smoker, I would have probably died of the stroke.

"Please, God, let me not die, so that I can see Neil and Tanja grow up! I must not worry them. The pain in my arm is unbearable. Now it is the same with my left leg. I cannot bear to put it down on the floor. I cannot even hop on my right one. I have no bounce!"

All these mixed thoughts crowded my mind. Is it just a momentary disaster or will I be a permanent gibbering invalid? I remember friends telling me about their parents who had had strokes and been left almost speechless and crippled for years, before second or third strokes finished them off. "Please, God, let me live!" At last, something positive to grasp! "I don't care how long it takes, just let me live! Remember, God, I am a fighter! I didn't escape death as a child, to die now while my children are still too young to be without me. The effect on both would be disastrous. And my beloved Graham. Has he not had enough worries over my health almost all our married life."

"What about the school? I cannot abandon my pupils when they are getting on so well. I cannot let the school down!"

"I've just called the doctor", Graham's calm voice reassured me. "He said he would be here in about an hour to an hour and a half."

At that moment, I suppose in a similar way to that in which a drowning person's life flashes through his brain, the substance of this book was born. I remember thinking about my mother and father, aunt Marga and uncle Rudi and all the other people who have made me what and who I am. About the lucky escapes from oblivion from which God had saved me, about the good fortune I have been blessed with and the bad times I had overcome and about the unknown future if, indeed, there was one. At whatever cost, as always, I determined to fight another battle.

Dr Bishop came at around 7 am, took my blood pressure and we all realised the reason for my stroke. The stress of the last day, possibly my over-reaction to the fight in the quadrangle, had caused my blood pressure to go over the top, in the same way that a surge in electricity causes a blown light bulb.

The doctor gave me two tablets to bring my blood pressure down and advised Graham to pour me my favourite alcoholic drink as, apparently, alcohol makes the blood vessels dilate, which would help the passage of any clots, if these were the cause of the stroke. He said he would return at lunchtime.

When the Doctor had gone, we began to discuss what I would like to drink. I do not like many alcoholic drinks and my favourite, shandy, would hardly do the trick. Finally, I settled for a cherry brandy in a wine glass. This was breakfast! Still, it was for medicinal purposes, was it not?

. Tanja woke up to go to school but was, understandably, frightened. She made herself ready, had breakfast, shouted 'Goodbye' and was off to catch her train to school. However, during the morning she telephoned Graham at work and asked how I was. He told her I was better.

Suddenly, while Graham was downstairs, I had to go to the bathroom. Hearing me call his father, Neil came into our bedroom and offered to help me. Very gently he made me lean on him and use him instead of my left leg, which I could not put down on the floor. Thus, still in great pain, I managed to get to the bathroom and back.

He was 18 and better able to accept illness than Tanja at the time.

I lay in bed unable to move all the morning, occasionally dozing off and hoping each time I would wake up well and whole again. However, this was not to be. Not yet, anyway. Amazingly, I never lost consciousness after the stroke.

At the time, Graham was working at Epping Branch and had to go to work, but Mrs Golding was coming that day to help with the housework and she was in the house during the morning. I certainly appreciated having her here that day.

Graham's arrival home at lunch time was shortly followed by Dr Bishop's. The latter took my blood pressure again and shook his head. "I'm sorry, but your blood pressure is exactly the same as this morning. The tablets have made no difference. You will have to go to hospital."

Instead of alarming me, the news that I will have to go to hospital calmed and reassured me. After all, there they had many ways of lowering blood pressure or dealing with another stroke and if, God forbid, I was paralysed, they could do something, surely.

After very painfully negotiating the stairs, Graham drove me to the hospital straight away. The descent of the stairs must have taken me half an hour.

Before I went into hospital, Graham telephoned the secretary at Tanja's school and asked her to break the news to Tanja gently that I was goint in to hospital, but that there was no danger to my life. The secretary very kindly took her aside and told her the facts. Tanja told us later that she was offered tea or coffee with the secretary and when she refused that or a drink of orange, the latter suggested a glass of sherry to help with the shock. As Tanja had never had an alcoholic drink, this surprised, but did not tempt her. We were very grateful when we realised how well this lady had handled the situation.

When we arrived at the Casualty Department, my blood pressure was extremely high and, as they were expecting us, I thought I would be rushed through, so that treatment could commence. How wrong I was!

A very pleasant young nurse chatted to me for a couple of hours, telling me how her uncle had died of a heart attack in the street. Also, how her father or grandfather had also had a heart attack or a stroke, she could not remember which. I was grateful she talked to me, but made a mental note to ask someone who trains nurses to tell them to choose their topics of conversation carefully, otherwise they might do more harm than good with their idle chatter!

The medical houseman, a very charming young doctor, then interviewed and tested me, prescribing treatment for when I eventually reached the ward. More talk about death and family from the pleasant young nurse. Graham, of course, had gone back to work as soon as he settled me on the trolley in A & E Department.

At last, nearly five hours after admission, I found myself in Harvey Ward, which was to be my home for about two months. In a way, I suppose, I was lucky this all happened in 1978; had it happened nowadays, a wait of many more hours might have been expected. On the other hand, there have been great strides in stroke rehabilitation. The medical establishment state now that it is vital to treat stroke patients as soon as possible, in order to save more brain cells from dying.

The nurses started preparing me for a drip. "But I am not to have a drip", I protested.

"Yes, you are. Don't argue." The drip was being brought in.

"Doctor did not say I am to have a drip. Please don't give me a drip. I am to have an injection of . . . to bring my diastolic blood pressure to below 100."

"What is your name? It is Mrs W . . . , isn't it?"

"No, it is NOT! I am Mrs Peacock."

"Oh, sorry! The drip is for Mrs W . . ."

"That's all right." At last, five hours after reaching hospital and nearly twenty hours after the initial stroke, I am to have the injection I need and have my blood pressure monitored. I suddenly saw a girl I used to teach typing in student nurse's uniform. A familiar face was smiling at me and I felt happier.

From then on I had my blood pressure taken frequently and, thank goodness, it fell after the first injection and tablets. However, the paralysis in my arm and leg became steadily worse over the next two days, until my arm and hand felt like a dead piece of meat. I could pick up my left hand with my right and just drop it on to the bed like a dead weight. By then I could not walk at all. However, I was still very cheerful, much to everyone's surprise. I suppose, I was just so happy to be alive.

In other large hospitals, such as the Charing Cross in London, doctors attend to stroke patients immediately and treat them as soon as possible, in order to arrest the increasing paralysis, which occurs within 24 hours or so.

The next evening Graham came to see me. He brought me a beautiful letter from Tanja, begging my forgiveness and taking the full blame for my stroke, because of her argument with Neil the night before. I wrote back, saying that it was not her fault at all, of course, but I did appreciate the letter. It was probably the fright I received when I saw the incident in the quad, or just fate. Certainly my blood pressure was quite normal prior to then, as I had had it checked by the doctor earlier that month.

I don't know how so many people heard so quickly about my misfortune, but I was very lucky to receive numerous flowers, cards and miniature gardens in dishes, some of which still grace our living room and with which I would not part. Stewards and Leventhorpe schools, King Harold School, everyone with whom I had ever taught seemed to be so generous and thoughtful when I needed it most.

In the bed next to me was a wonderful old lady, Molly, who was an inspiration to me. She was the widow of a Bank Manager, full of energy and only in hospital to stabilise her diabetic condition. She arranged everyone's flowers, helped to cover me at night when I could not do it myself but, most of all, she cheered everyone up. It is rather sad to think that, although she was discharged long before me, she had to return to hospital and, apparently, died a year or two afterwards from something serious like cancer.

The nursing care under the able direction of Sister Fiona MacMorrow was excellent, but half my time, after about the first three days, was spent being treated, or rather working hard on rehabilitation in the Physiotherapy Department. It is to the cheerfulness, professionalism and general air of 'we know you can do it' of the members of that Department that I owe my recovery from a massive left stroke.

After the first shock when, just for a minute or so I despaired of ever making a proper recovery, I hoped that I would recover enough to go back to school during that school year. No one would commit himself or herself when answering my question whether I would recover sufficiently to work again as a secondary school teacher, whether of Commerce, English, German or Drama.

It is a pity that there was so little information known about the physical feelings or sensations of post stroke patients. I had many peculiar sensations, which I mentioned to the doctors, particularly the charming houseman, Dr Taylor, whom everyone adored, but no one knew whether every stroke patient felt any of them.

From observing and talking to stroke patients, I would conclude that nearly all feel happiest when they have closed their eyes. For many years afterwards I still enjoyed closing my eyes and 'letting go'.

The other sensation was feeling as if there was a stiff board dividing the left and right sides of my head. The right half felt normal, while the left felt as if it was filled with cavity foam insulation. The left side of my face would also feel as if it was burning from high fever.

I would be very cheerful most of the time, particularly when it was visiting time, but somehow I could not cope with more than one or two faces at a time. I was probably afraid that the excitement might raise my blood pressure, but it never did; the tablets saw to that. I never minded having my blood pressure taken very often and very regularly, as I felt this would prevent another stroke. Any upward variation would thus be checked before it was out of control.

RING-A-ROUND

Needles and pins-a
Needles and pins-a
Thus the song entones,
These are life-and-death-a
Feel them in my bones!

Sudden numbness, sudden pain,
Will I ever walk again?

God in heaven, is this the end?
Please have mercy, be my friend.

My arm feels heavy, my face dead!
Is this a stroke, need I dread?

My reason's lucid, my speech clear,
I'm so lucky, sight's still here!

Crisis has passed, the damage done,
Let's count my blessings, every one:

I can see clearly, that's best of all,
I have my mind and can recall.

What's more, I hear as good as new
All around, melodious and true.

When many weeks of work are done
I'll walk as well as anyone.

It's true, my grip is not as strong,
But wait, it will be before long!

Every minute I spend in bed
There's music going through my head.

I wake up joyous to be alive,
With song in heart and then I thrive.

My husband's waiting at the gate
An extra blessing, now I have eight!

To see my children grow so tall
Bonus and best blessing of all.

The ring's complete, new life's begun
I'm whole again, let's all move on!

(Written in hospital after the stroke
that occurred Friday, 13 October 1978)

Dr Medley was an excellent consultant and I was very grateful to be his patient; I really feel that he saved my life. He also seemed to appreciate the fact that I was pushing myself to the best of my ability, in order to make as much progress as possible.

The worst sensation I ever experienced was late one night when I could not lie down. I could barely breathe without stifling a scream of pain. There seemed to be another board dividing my body on the left hand side, horizontally back to front from just below the shoulder blade to the ribs. I wondered what it could be and whether I would ever get rid of the excruciating pain. Then suddenly it struck me that it could be that all the internal stitching and scarring from the kidney excision could be affected by the stroke. I asked the doctor, who had been called by this time and he agreed that this is what it probably was. Whether he really believed this or not I shall never know, but it seemed to satisfy me at the time.

Man is a peculiar animal. He can bear pain or anything else, as long as there is some logical and rational explanation. It is the unknown, the unexpected and the unexplained, which he fears most.

Every day Patrick, the Physiotherapy Department's cheerful porter, would come to Harvey Ward to fetch his charges. We would get into the wheelchairs and he would push us into the lift, to alight on the ground floor and be taken to Physiotherapy.

One fact I nearly forgot to mention. Dr Medley put me on a strict diet of 600 calories, as he felt I would recover more quickly if I had less weight to carry. Since I had the kidney removed, I had put on a lot of weight and this did not help. However, the tiredness I felt most of the time, whether it was due to the stroke or the tablets I was taking, was intensified by the poor diet prescribed to help me lose weight. I could think of nothing but food and implored Graham to bring me mushroom salad to complement my meals. There are no calories in mushrooms soaked in lemon juice.

Everyone around me was choosing succulent dishes from the menu, while I had boiled fish and carrots or half a slice of ham, quarter of a tomato and a lettuce leaf. The best meal of the day was breakfast, which consisted of half a grapefruit and a soft- boiled egg. Or it would have been the best meal of the day, had I been able to undo the clingfilm round the grapefruit and cut the segments through with one hand. Help usually came in the form of Tina, the cleaner, who was always there when I needed help to get to the grapefruit. Eventually, Mrs Bell-Jones, the Physiotherapist who specialised in strokes and who was very dedicated, sent a message to the doctors:

"Mrs Peacock must eat more, as she is too hungry, too tired and too weak to cope with physiotherapy."

Hooray! I could have 800 calories per day; a whole slice of brown bread for breakfast with an egg, plus other goodies, in moderation.

My first sight of the large Physiotherapy room was very depressing and awe-inspiring at the same time. It was depressing, because the first patient I saw had no legs and looked very pathetic with his eyes closed, but trying to move across a mattress. I could hardly stop my tears from flowing and felt that the sights I saw, far from making me feel better, would raise my blood pressure. Later, when I met and came to know that patient, I knew that he was one of the jolliest, most talented and gregarious persons I had ever met. It just goes to show that first appearances can be deceptive.

I was placed on the mattress with sandbags across my left hand and left foot. They were placed in such a way that my foot would stay down and my hand would remain open, for a 'stroked' hand's inclination is to remain clenched. On one side of me I had the physiotherapist explaining how I would get better daily, while on the other side, on that first day I had 'Bill'. He was a middle-aged man, who had been involved in a horrific car accident and was now completely speechless and appeared to have the mind of a baby. His legs were always drawn up and that morning, as I believe every morning for the previous three months, the physiotherapists were trying to get him to straighten his legs. I was afraid that he would roll onto me, but realised later that he could not and managed to relax.

I said that I was awe-inspired, too, on that first day in the Physiotherapy hall, as indeed on many other days. The dedication and inspiration in the faces of all the people working in the departments, as well as the effort made by all the patients, or at least most of them, caused me to feel awed. Sometimes it must seem very boring to the ladies to have to start therapy on yet another stroke patient, but they never show it. Each patient is made to feel special and worth the effort. This certainly communicated itself to the patients and we, too, then tried to make a special effort, in order to make their work worthwhile.

The friends I made in that room, both with the patients and staff, I remember with fondness and they will always have a special place in my album of memories. Some of the treatment, such as walking up and down on a board placed on a cylinder and not losing my balance, I managed to do quite early on, whilst touching the top of my head slowly with my left palm without dropping my hand like a ton of bricks and knocking myself out came much later. Solving a jig-saw puzzle, picking up the pieces with my left hand only, I managed to do after several weeks, much to my joy. On the other hand, climbing the wall bars with my hands, one at a time, was more difficult.

I was intrigued every day to see several patients, particularly a young girl who had suffered a stroke as a result of a serious heart operation, undergo some kind of electrical treatment and was both afraid and hopeful at the same time that this might be offered to me. I had always been afraid of electric shocks - who has not - and was sure that if I had ever been mentally ill, I would have refused ECT.

One morning, the day I had waited for and dreaded, Mrs Clarke, another physiotherapist, suggested that, as my fingers were still inclined to be clenched all the time and I found it difficult to move them, I should let her try the electric treatment. I just could not believe that it did not hurt but, as I found to my surprise and joy, it does not. A wet bandage is placed round the arm, with a contact embedded in it, then the other electrode is placed on various points of the arm and wrist. When certain nerves are touched, the fingers involuntarily open up. When one's fingers have been tightly clenched together and then suddenly one sees them splayed out, even if it was done artificially, one gets a vision of normality and future possibility of a cure. This certainly gives the patient hope and will to carry on with any treatment, which may bring the damage or illness to an end.

Once this particular treatment was started, I could hardly wait every day for my turn to have it. I felt that if the electricity could stimulate my fingers, surely there was hope! When, occasionally, other patients had this treatment and there was not enough time left for me to have the same, I would get very upset at the unfairness of it, though I could not let anyone know this.

The only drawback to physiotherapy was the return to the ward. For some reason, stroke robs its victims of patience. Even a two-minute wait for attention seems like an hour to a person who has suffered a stroke. Therefore, as soon as we had been told: "Enough for today", and wheeled to the end of the corridor, ready to be returned to the ward by Patrick, in strict rotation, the worst time of the day for us began and our disability seemed to become almost overwhelming.

Once back in the ward, reading, talking or just resting, life was bearable again. I was always keen on keeping busy and this time was no exception. The occupational therapist had managed to buy me an embroidery frame, which could be fixed on to a little table and I was, therefore, overjoyed that I could sit in a chair and embroider tray cloths, thus feeling useful again. My output, of course, nowhere nearly equalled that from Honey Lane days, but it was a start. Physiotherapy always took place in the morning and I was delivered back to the ward in time for lunch. Therefore, there was plenty of time for embroidery and reading.

One other activity during my post stroke recovery in hospital, which always took place in the afternoon and which I still remember with horror, was having a bath. All my life up till then I loved having baths, but never do I now approach bathing without an air of trepidation and unwillingness, though I must admit this is beginning to wear off, thank goodness. If cleanliness is next to godliness, patients in hospitals must be very godly. I am sure that, as soon as some nurses said: "What shall we do next?", the answer was invariably: "Give Mrs Peacock a bath."

The bane of my life and the cause of my trepidation and unease was the chair lift used to lift naked patients and immerse them in the bath. I must have looked like a Buddha on a throne ready to be sacrificed in the holy river, the first time I sat in the chair lift and waited for my dip. Being strapped in the chair, lifted in the air, immersed, soaped, washed, lifted out, dried, powdered, etc, never actually hurt, so the only reason I can think of for my total dread and discomfort when faced with the prospect of a bath, must have been due to the indignity I felt at not being able to get out of the wheelchair and place myself in the bathtub. Perhaps it was the fact that when I compared the nurses' young, firm and vital bodies with my own old and broken one, I felt ashamed and wanted to hide. On the other hand, I might have been reminded of my shaming showers in prison.

Only a few days after I was admitted to hospital, I was taken in my wheelchair to the Occupational Therapists' room and asked to try to dress myself, especially given my bra to fasten at the back. What stupidity! Here was I, less than a week after a serious stroke, still to be confined to hospital for nearly two months, yet required to demonstrate my ability to dress myself! The fact that I could not possibly do up a bra or put a blouse on really upset me and made me think that I would never be able to do these things by myself. How much more sensible would it have been to ask me to demonstrate any of this just before I was discharged, instead of then? In my suggestions on leaving hospital I emphasised this.

After a few weeks in hospital, when my blood pressure was stable and I was making "excellent progress", according to the medical profession, I was allowed home for a day on Sunday and for a weekend after that.

The first time Dr Medley gave me permission to go, I was terrified. A whole day without having my blood pressure taken! It could not be raised greatly, apparently, while I was on tablets, I was assured yet again. As there was no physiotherapy at weekends, I knew I would not miss any of that or the electrical treatment.

Graham wheeled me to the lift and down to the car. I could walk hesitatingly, limping badly, on his arm on later visits, but was quite happy to be going home even in a wheelchair. Soon we were home to Neil and Tanja. I did not realise how much I missed being with them. It is true, they visited me regularly, but hospital visits are not very natural. Even the first few hours at home with them were not natural, but gradually, when they stopped treating me like Dresden china or like a welcome visitor, I knew I was accepted and part of the family again.

Eventually, after eight weeks, just before Christmas, I was discharged and advised that I should go to physiotherapy three times a week. Many patients were collected by ambulance and it seemed a good idea to have an ambulance collect me at about 8.30 am or 9 am, as it already had to collect another patient in the neighbourhood.

Monday came and Graham helped me to get ready for 8.25 am. I waited expectantly.8.30 came and passed. The same can be said for 9 o'clock and 10 o'clock. As I mentioned before, impatience to an unbelievable, almost dangerous degree is the penalty for having a stroke. At 10.30, I telephoned the Physiotherapy Department and enquired what had happened? The ambulance had a flat tyre and could not come.

Another was sent, but this had a different defect and returned empty. They would try to send a third, but not to worry. I could come on Wednesday. When no transport turned up, I was in a state. Would I seize up and regress if I had no physiotherapy from Friday to Wednesday? Would all my progress to date have been in vain? What about my blood pressure? Would it be greatly raised as I was so upset and had no patience any more? I, who always used to be incredibly patient! What was the effect on the other stroke patients, to whom this might happen at least once a week? No ambulance turned up on Wednesday either. At least none turned up at this end. To add insult to injury, Mrs Clarke told me later that an ambulance turned up at the hospital at 1 o'clock to take me back home!

I always felt very sorry from then on for the other stroke patients who had to rely on ambulances to be collected for physiotherapy. I had opted never to put myself in that position again, but to go with Graham at 7.30 am and wait in the foyer of the hospital until Physiotherapy Department opened and was ready to receive patients at around 9.30 am. At least I could read the newspaper or do a crossword. When I was finished at midday, Graham picked me up in his lunch hour and took me home.

After several weeks of going three times per week, I was down to twice, then once a week and, eventually, was told that I need not come again, but could exercise at home. I did not feel ready to give up the support of the Department, but realised that it was useless to argue and that it was with my best interests at heart that they signed me off.

The crutch of the hospital is hard to give up for some patients, but it must be surmounted if the patient is to make real progress, if at all possible. Besides, there were new stroke patients whose need was as great as mine had been, in addition to many Multiple Sclerosis victims of all ages, who would always have to come. Also, I would be freer to invite people round or to go out with friends. After all, Dr. Hamilton would still keep a kind and watchful eye over my blood pressure. The strength of the tablets had now been reduced from 40 mg per tablet to 10 mg and my blood pressure was now normal.

At first when I went out by myself I could not go far, without having to sit down. I limped quite badly, though I realised how lucky I was to be walking at all. At the same time, subconsciously, I became afraid to go out by myself. The short downhill walk to the bus stop seemed like a huge mountain to conquer. Whether this was the result of the stroke or hospitalisation I did not know, but I am sure that if I had not faced it and made myself go out as often as I could, summoning up all the energy and courage of which I was capable, I could easily have developed agrophobia. Each time I left the safety of the home in those early days to go to the bus stop and the Town Centre, I felt terrified; my head would thump and I felt a constriction in my throat. It would have been so easy to turn back, but I went forward partly for my own sake, but mostly, I think, for the sake of my family and all the people at the hospital who had helped me.

I usually believe in sharing my feelings and worries with my family and friends, just as I believe in sharing their feelings and problems. However, I never confided these particular fears to anyone until now.

The reasons for my reluctance were twofold: in the first instance, I did not want to worry Graham, for he had had more than his fair share of worry during our lifetime together and, secondly, particularly where Neil and Tanja were concerned, I wanted them to consider me as 'normal' as possible, just like most mothers. I was very much aware that physical defects somehow seem abhorrent to children and I did not want to be considered 'a cripple'. I wanted love from them, not pity. I had heard of adolescent and grown up children not going home to visit after one parent had had a stroke or, if going home, ignoring that fact.

Nearly nine months after the stroke I realised that it was foolish of me to think I could go back to full time teaching as I was. I felt very sleepy a lot of the time and had to rest. Whereas all my life previously I was always busy - I could never do less than two or three jobs at once, never walked but always ran, as if I was just about to miss a bus - now I had to take things easy.

I remembered ruefully Leslie always telling me to slow down. He explained, and I often think of his words now and reflect how true they were, that life was like a roll of cloth: there was only a finite length of it on the roll; your life depended on how you used the cloth. If you used a lot of it fast, you will come to the end of the roll quickly. If you lived at a slower pace, the roll will last longer. I, therefore, determined to be a full time housewife and not hanker after outside work. After all, ordinary tasks, such as peeling potatoes, now took me much longer than before. The people in Physiotherapy also advised me at the time of leaving hospital that I will not be able to make strides on the way to full recovery unless I resigned my teaching position, as I was still worrying about the progress of my pupils. Therefore, reluctantly, I sent my notice to Essex County Council, as I also felt guilty to be in receipt of even half pay while unable to teach. This, unfortunately, caused me to lose my pension, but speeded my recovery.

I did investigate the possibility of becoming a part time Speech Therapy Aide, working with handicapped children or even training as a Speech Therapist. While I was still attending Physiotherapy, I occasionally tried to help Bill or one of the other patients who, due to a right side stroke had lost their speech and as I seemed to have a small degree of success, I felt that perhaps if I could not teach any more, I could be useful in this field. I imagined that some of my qualifications would exempt me from part of a Speech Therapist's training. Unfortunately, I would have had to start training from the beginning for a Speech Therapist and felt that, in my condition, that would have been too taxing. In addition, there were no vacancies for

Therapist Aides, even on a voluntary basis.

Then a curious phenomenon occurred. The minute I resigned and the pressure was off me to regain enough health to resume teaching, I became more alert and decided to face the future, however short or long, with equanimity and hope.

CHAPTER 9
There Is Life After Stroke

My life suddenly became divided into BMS and AMS, as I found myself prefacing quite a lot of my conversation with the words 'Before My Stroke' or 'After My Stroke', until I realised that, although physically I might not be able to do all the things I used to be able to do or took longer over them, I was basically the same person with the same faults and the same good qualities as before. Therefore, there was no reason for me to make excuses for the way that I was.

When Stewards School needed an English teacher for the summer term in 1980, I accepted a term's work, having already taught there for two weeks in the spring, just to 'test the waters'.

It was wonderful to be back in a Staff-room amongst friends and even better to teach youngsters who had had many changes of teacher in the previous two terms. They appreciated stability and I appreciated the challenge and the opportunity. Since then I have taught on supply at several schools, including King Harold. I was a little afraid of going back there, in view of the fact that I was teaching there when I had the stroke, but after one day the ghost was laid and I had taught there for five months when I wrote the bulk of the first MS of this book.

Since then, until 1998, when I was 68, I taught on supply for many weeks and months at a time at several schools in Harlow and Loughton, a great part full time. I loved every minute, particularly, my time at Mark Hall, St Mark's, Stewards, Passmores, Brays Grove and Loughton County High School for Girls, where again I made many friends. The subjects I enjoyed teaching most were English, Drama, German, French, Commerce and Typewriting. It is a pity Keyboard skill is not universally taught nowadays.

It gives me great joy when I meet young people around Harlow, who come over and tell me that the love of learning foreign languages and my enthusiasm instilled in them a love of another language, particularly if they have then studied that language at University, as many of them have. Recently, I also met a girl with two teenage boys of her own who told me that my insistence on learning touch-typing led her to a good job in the city and that she will be eternally grateful to me for my perseverance in not letting her waste her time, despite her attitude in class! And she was one of the best behaved, I thought! I remembered her class very well, as they were the first year of the ROSLA (Raising of School Leaving Age from 15 - 16) generation and quite difficult in my very first year of teaching; some of them were there under protest, as they would much rather have been out at work, they said.

Between 1980 and 1983 Tanja was very ill and, unfortunately, had to be hospitalised several times for many weeks but, like me, she is a fighter. She was very brave when, despite her illness and having to stay in hospital, she sat her 'O' levels and passed them well. Throughout those dark days we hoped and prayed that she would be cured and would end up a happy, contented and fulfilled young lady who showed such promise for life at an early age.

Neil, after an initial hiccup of not obtaining all the high grades needed for University, obtained them in the first three months of his gap year and then worked the rest of the year before joining Loughborough University, where he obtained an Honours degree in Economics and Social Psychology. He enjoyed life to the full, according to him, playing a lot of sport. He went up to Buckingham Palace on 1 June 1982 to receive his Gold Duke of Edinburgh Award from Prince Philip. My joy knows no bounds when I see what good friends Neil and Tanja have become.

Graham and I celebrated our Silver Wedding anniversary in July 1981. Tanja came out of hospital at the end of June, soon after she had sat her 'O' levels; She immediately made us a wonderful two tier wedding cake and supervised the preparations for two parties to celebrate the event. The first was a cheese and wine party on a weekday evening in the garden, to which all our friends from Finchmoor and Burnett Park were invited. This was a great occasion as well as the warmest night of the year. Everyone seemed to enjoy the party and all our friends mixed well.

The following Sunday we had all our very close friends and family to a Garden Party meal and we all enjoyed it immensely. People whom we had not seen for twenty years came and it seemed as if time had stood still.

Both these occasions reaffirmed our love and good fortune to have each other and our family and friends. Neil worked ceaselessly as barman at both gatherings, while Tanja acted as co-hostess and also recited the doggerel verse I had written to celebrate our twenty-five years together.

In the summer of 1982, the year some of this book was originally written, Tanja and I went youth-hostelling in Cornwall. It was therapeutic for both of us and, although it was four years since my stroke, when no more improvement should have taken place, the final vestiges of my limp disappeared and I am very grateful to Tanja for the walks around Newquay that caused this to happen.

I was not aware myself of this miracle, until I started teaching again in the autumn. Some children in the playground stopped me: "Mrs Peacock, you used to limp, but now you don't! What happened?" Would they have believed me had I told them that, indeed, once again I had had a miraculous cure and recovery. The hospital had told me that a stroke patient can recover for up to two years after the event, but not later. Yet I had been improving up to four years afterwards or maybe even more.

It is said that each experience we undergo or survive teaches us something, whether the experience is pleasant or unpleasant. The fact that we become different afterwards is indisputable. For instance, people have 'chips' on their shoulders after being slighted by not receiving an honour that they thought they deserved, or people become mean after becoming rich. Whether, if the experience is unpleasant or life threatening, it also makes us better people, I am not sure.

What have I, learnt from my experiences? The most important principle is the fact that no one should ever take anything for granted, particularly not good health, happiness, families or jobs. These are all bounties to be appreciated.

At the basic level, I have learnt that food is precious and often I find it hard to throw away any left overs which might 'come in useful', particularly bread. I can never also pass by a beggar or busker, without giving something, even a small coin. I often buy too much food, in case we run short or someone comes to visit and we have nothing suitable to offer. Graham teases me by saying: "If there's ever a shortage of anything, we'll be able to supply all the neighbourhood, won't we?"

At a higher level, I am sure I appreciate the beauty of nature and the finer things in life which money cannot buy. No one can purchase a baby's smile or the squeeze of a trusting hand in one's own. No one can buy the infinity and tranquillity of a starry night or the momentous first step taken into marriage by the bridal couple, when all their mysterious life together lays uncharted before them. However, most essential of all, I have learnt that physical possessions are not at all important. I am slowly teaching this particular wisdom to my family. If they lose some money, a gold necklace or break a piece of china, however precious, I always bully them to accept that 'Nothing is important, except health!"

Neil and Janet

**Our grandchildren - Sam, Joshua and Joe
born in 1993, 1999 and 1997 respectively**
(Neil and Janet's children)

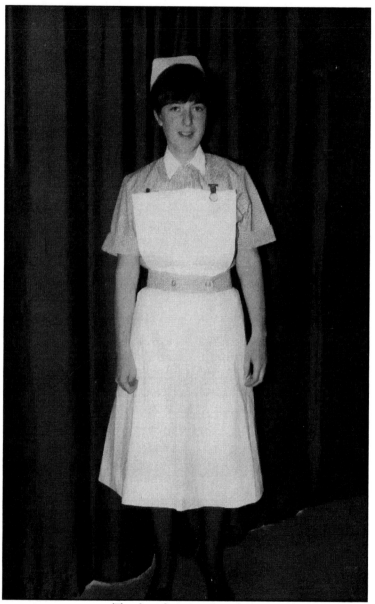

Tanja after graduation

Tanja

POSTSCRIPT

I am beginning to feel that there is always a purpose in any event which happens in life. Whenever we feel complacent, perhaps, something happens to shake that complacency.

For many years now I have always practised counting my blessings before going to bed at night. Even when things have seemed very gloomy, just after my stroke, or when Tanja was desperately ill and we did not know which way to turn, I still counted my blessings. My belief in God wavered very little. However, I remember one Sunday afternoon, when I was worried out of my mind about Tanja's health and chance of recovery, I went into the kitchen and said to myself out loud: "There can't be a God. He would not let us suffer so much!" And yet, I walked straight into another room, dropped on my knees and sent up a fervent prayer to Him, both a prayer for forgiveness and of supplication.

I do not expect I will ever regain the speed of 110 words per minute on the keyboard, which I used to be able to do accurately for five minutes before the stroke. That would have been really useful now that I needed to retype and revise this manuscript on my computer.

When I think of the number of manuscripts and theses I used to type for anyone in need, this makes me a little sad. However, think positive! I could have been dead so many times. I could have been crippled, lost my speech, been wheelchair bound. I have a wonderful family, the result of that chance encounter at Waterloo Station. Was it chance? I can do everything else, but type at speed, even play the piano again, though no better than before the stroke! I have regularly taught until 1998 at secondary schools in the district on supply and now I do mentoring at a school which I greatly enjoy and which, apparently, the youngsters I mentor also enjoy. Who needs typing at great speed anyway?

Just as I finished writing the first draft of this book, my doctor informed me that I had become diabetic. Luckily, I did not have to have injections or tablets at the time, but only had to be careful what I had to eat. On hearing the news of my latest illness, my son said he was very sorry, but he was sure it was all a publicity stunt for the book! My daughter said: "Thank Goodness, Mum, it is nothing more serious!"

EPILOGUE

The most curious feature of writing this book was the fact that, as soon as I started writing it one day in my lunch hour at school, I wrote steadily every free moment I had and then for three weeks solidly the following Easter holiday. I did not have to plan or think what I was going to write. Events, incidents and occasions just sorted themselves automatically in chronological order, completely amazing me, until I completed the final page. Then the hand-written manuscript, mostly written in an old exercise book, lay untouched and mislaid for several years, as if waiting for me to regain my typing skill or inherit Graham's computer and complete a Silver Surfers' course.

I wrote at the time when I found the script that my happiness was nearly complete. Graham had been promoted to the job to which he aspired since joining the bank, that of a Bank Manager and enjoyed his work more than at any other time in his life. Tanja, then, after working for eighteen months in the Pathology Laboratory at Princess Alexandra Hospital in Harlow had just completed nearly three years of a four year RGN/RSCN course as a student nurse at Great Ormond Street Hospital for Sick Children and University College Hospital, both in London. Neil had obtained his BSc (Hons) degree and had been working in a job he enjoyed for a few years. He had also met Janet at University and they were buying a house jointly in Milton Keynes. We had warmly welcomed Janet into our family and Tanja, at last, had a 'sister' of whom she is justly fond.

Unfortunately, also during that time, Graham had had to have two small operations on his face, one of which was cosmetic, while the other was to remove a tiny cancerous spot, but he had been reassured that it was nothing to worry about in future. Perhaps he just wanted to be in fashion, like President Reagan at the time!

As well as facial surgery, he also had extensive surgery on one of his knees, due to a malignant mole, but it was all done in time, thank God.

Now, many years later still, I have taken up and revised this manuscript, brought it up to date and completely retyped it on the computer, in order to to have it published. I hope it'll make interesting reading. Coupled with Graham's research into his family's history, it will be a record for our family's posterity.

Although I managed to control my diabetes for about 14 years purely by diet, in the last few years I have had to supplement this with a diabetic tablet per day. Unfortunately, because I take this tablet and it reacts with one of the tablets I have to take for high blood pressure, I found that I could not continue teaching, as I had to have lunch promptly at about 12 noon. In any case, I carried on far beyond the usual retirement age!

. Graham has been retired from the Bank for ten years, since he was 60, but for the last 13 years has managed the British Disabled Alpine Ski Team and the Paralympic Ski Team, as well as being a Director of British Paralympic Association. He has also qualified as a Ski Instructor, both for the able-bodied and the disabled. As Team Manager, he has attended The Winter Paralympic Games in 1992, 1994, 1998 and 2002, in Tignes-Albertville (France), Lillehammer (Norway), Nagano (Japan) and Salt Lake City (Utah, America), respectively. These voluntary jobs have certainly kept him busy and, during the winter months very fit, skiing in the mountains, though the administration was almost full time work. He has now given up managing the team, although he is still quite involved with it.

At the same time, I have been Publicity Officer for National Handicapped Skiers' Association and have published a regular Newsletter called The Summit. I also worked at the French Paralympics in 1992 for the organisers, translating daily weather forecasts into English, which I enjoyed immensely. In fact, I liked the subject so much that, had I been younger, I feel sure I would have taken up Meteorology as a career! Attending the Norwegian Paralympics and several World Championships, both in Europe and in America was also very exciting.

The children have moved on and we are very proud of them both. Tanja attended several Youth With a Mission courses in this country and in New Zealand, with outreach work in Canada and Indonesia. She also worked in a hospital in India for six weeks for the British Missionary Society, after qualification. She worked for several years as a Senior Paediatric Nurse Practitioner at a hospital in London, as well as working occasionally at the National Asthma Helpline, when they needed her, and did a part time Master's degree. She is an asthma specialist and also ran clinics at two hospitals. However, this year she left her job to work for a small Christian Charity involved with helping children affected by HIV and Aids. We are very proud of her dedication. In addition to playing the clarinet, the guitar, the piano and all the recorders, she has learnt to play the saxophone in a year and then passed Grade VI, with distinction.

Neil is Financial Director of a large Multi-National Company. In his spare time, he trains his sons' school football team, referees and also plays lead guitar in a very good Rock and Roll band, called Dead Cat Bounce (a financial term for shares which go up or down unexpectedly; all the members work in the financial field). The band often plays at Society weddings, charitable events and similar occasions. He and Janet were married in 1991, at a beautiful wedding, where Tanja was the Chief Bridesmaid. They have three wonderful little boys, the most precious thing in all our lives: Samuel, born in 1993, Joseph (Joe), born in 1997 and Joshua, born in 1999.

Although I find I cannot walk too far without stopping and also have 'dodgy knees', I have taken up line dancing, aqua-aerobics and yoga, each once a week, and joined a writers' group, The Inn Scribers.

As well as writing poetry, I have been writing articles and entering competitions, whenever I have a spare moment from trying to raise money for National Handicapped Skiers' Association, with some success. I have had several poems published in anthologies and won second prize with a poem in Writers' Forum magazine. This year (2004), I had two one page articles published in My Weekly, one of which was commissioned.

In 2003, The Caravan Club advertised in its magazine for people who spoke several languages to get in touch with them and, perhaps, be appointed Overseas Site Inspectors. Much to everyone's surprise, they had about 550 replies. This they whittled down to 14 couples. We were delighted to be chosen as one of those.

Last year, therefore, Graham and I visited Croatia on behalf of the Caravan Club, in order to find suitable campsites between Split and Dubrovnik, for the Club to take a party of caravanners there this year. They seemed to be delighted with our detailed reports on four of these. Therefore, this year Graham and I ran a rally for them in Dubrovnik, which was very successful and prepared site inspection visits in Germany and Austria. We have also attended a course on travel writing and are hoping to have some articles published.

Life is too precious to waste!

THE CHILDREN OF BOSNIA

(Croat, Muslim and Serb, but
this applies equally to the
children of Kosovo)

The eyes have it! Windows of the soul
Reflect their human hunger, their goal
No further than the next First Aid bus.
What wouldn't they give to be one of us?

They have perfect sight, but cannot see
An end to despair and misery.
Where is the warmth of familiar touch,
Which in the past always meant so much?

We hear their cries, their so urgent need,
Yet we don't seem to pay them full heed.
There are folk still who ignore their pain,
With 'Charity starts at home' refrain.

Wake up, humanity, we can do more,
We all must answer this knock at our door.
Life is precious, easily brought to its end -
Save the children and our dignity, my friend!

Verica Peacock

POST-POSTSCRIPT
13 October 2003

Today is the day I thought would never come. Not some exciting, long planned happening or the day I might have won the lottery, though I'm deliriously happy. I feel like I have won a prize, the highest stakes, the biggest lottery prize, my life, for today is the 25th anniversary of the day I had a massive stroke. Unplanned, unprepared, it struck stealthily in the middle of the night, paralysing me all the way down my left side, yet I was only 48 years old.

I feel I have been given a new lease of life, working for the Caravan Club for a week or two during the Summer months, particularly in the country of my birth and meeting so many new people of all nationalities, who turn out to be dear friends.

I am nearly 74, but today I feel very lucky and blessed to have been allowed to survive so long, first of all the Holocaust, then a nearly fatal stroke, in order to enjoy my family, the company of so many friends, my writing and what is left of my life. There is still so much more I hope I will be able to accomplish!

THANKS

I know this part of a book is usually trite and boring to the readers but, nevertheless, I wanted to include my heartfelt thanks to all my numerous friends and family for their unfailing help and encouragement, whenever I needed it most during the past half century, to all the children I have ever taught, for I never felt happier and more alive than when I was teaching (except for my very first two lessons); to John Evans for reading and re-reading the first attempted manuscript for me, in order to make some suggestions for additions; to all the doctors, nurses and physiotherapists who helped me cope with illnesses and set-backs, encouraging my progress, particularly Drs Gordon, Hamilton, Medley, Rhys-Jones and Mr Barron; to Mesdames Bell-Jones, Clarke, Marsden, Marshall, Hughes and many others too numerous to mention, without whom I probably would not have been able to survive, let alone flourish! Unfortunately, some have since died and I have lost touch with others, but I still think of them with gratitude and affection.

To Jenny and Ivan and all my colleagues, friends and neighbours, both past and present.

The greatest, most patient and valuable help came, of course, from Graham, Tanja and Neil.

November 2004